Copyright © 1998 by
University Press of America,® Inc.
4720 Boston Way
Lanham, Maryland 20706

12 Hid's Copse Rd.
Cummor Hill, Oxford OX2 9JJ

Library of Congress Cataloging-in-Publication Data

Hali, Awelkhan.
Kazakh traditions of China / Awelkhan Hali, Zengxiang Li, Karl W.
Luckert.
p.   cm.
Includes bibliographical references and index.
1. Kazakhs—China—Sinkiang Uighur Autonomous Region—
History. 2. Kazakhs—China—Sinkiang Uighur Autonomous
Region—Social life and customs. 3. Sinkiang Uighur Antonomous
Region (China)—Ethnic relations. I. Li, Tseng-hsiang. II. Luckert,
Karl W. III. Title.
DS731.K38H35   1997   951'.600494345—DC21   97-40187 CIP

ISBN 0-7618-0955-4 (cloth: alk. ppr.)
ISBN 0-7618-0956-2 (pbk: alk. ppr.)

To the memory of

Nyhmet Myngzhan 1922–1993
and
Mahmoud Abu Saud 1914–1993

Contents

Preface

When in 1986 Karl W. Luckert began traveling to China in search of partners for joint research in ethnology and history of religions, among Chinese minorities, Li Zengxiang, a professor of Turkic languages at Central Nationalities University, responded. Hu Tan, Chen Yongling, and Wei Cuiyi were benevolent superiors who opened paths for our cooperation.

A grant procured by Mahmoud Abu Saud, in 1988, has helped Awelkhan Hali and Li Zengxiang begin field investigations in the Ili Prefecture. Over the years, Awelkhan Hali became our point man in dealing with most of the Kazakh sources. He wrote much of the first draft in Chinese, while Li Zengxiang furnished introductory historical materials, and portions for the chapter on marriage. The latter also was our interpreter between Kazakh and Chinese materials, as well as between Chinese and English renditions. Luckert initially was responsible for instigating the project and for lead topics and questions that kept the team working in the same general direction. Later he rewrote and expanded the manuscript, and set type. Everything presented in this volume has been translated, renegotiated and rewritten several times, in various languages and scripts.

At the Chinese side, Muhtur Abilqaq and Wang Jianmin have read the manuscript and have given good advice, while at the American side Linda and Jeffrey Ruff have helped reading the proofs. Over the years, Luckert has had available the good linguistic help of graduate assistants at Southwest Missouri State University—Yu Zongqi, Wang Ganhui, Yu Fenglan, Hou Zhilin, and Zan Tongbin. For consultation provided by other colleagues we appreciatively mention Mahmoud Abu Saud, Shahin Gerami, and Wei Cuiyi. All the shortcomings that might have remained or crept into the book, in spite of the help rendered by these people, will ultimately have to be chalked up to the account of the American co-author—who humbly confesses that co-authoring this volume, across several language boundaries and political fault lines, has turned out to be a more difficult task than all of us have imagined at the outset. We strove for perfection, to finally conclude with the hope that our efforts might stimulate future interest in Kazakh traditions among other scholars.

    We especially thank numerous Kazakh resource persons, retainers, traditionalists, as well as scholars in the humanities field, for all the traditions and folklore they have cherished, learned, preserved, and shared. A book of this kind is not possible without incurring a significant debt to scholars and colleagues past and present.

Kazakh Traditions of China

Photographic Glimpses of Kazakh Life

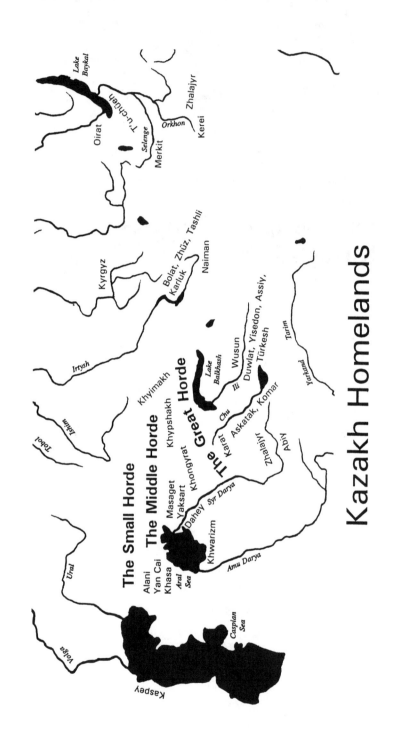

Kazakh Homelands

Lake Baykal

Oirat
T'u-chüeh
Selenge
Merkit
Orkhon
Zhalajyr
Kerei

Kyrgyz

Bolat, Zhüz, Tashii
Karluk
Naiman

Irtysh

Ishim
Tobol

Khyimakh

Wusun
Lake Balkhash
Ili
Duwlat, Yisedon, Assiy,
Türkesh
Tarim

The Middle Horde
Khypshakh
Chu
Askatak, Komar
Yarkand

The Small Horde
Khongyrat
The Great Horde
Karat
Zhalaiyr
AbiY

Masaget
Yaksart
Dahey   Syr Darya

Alani
Yan Cai
Khasa
Aral Sea
Khwarizm
Amu Darya

Ural

Volga
Kaspey
Caspian Sea

1. A small Kazakh boy struggles for the obedience of his horse.

2. An older boy dares his mount to run down a photographer who trusted the horse's common sense. Here, in White Poplar Valley (*Terekti Sai*), most Kazakhs belong to the Kerei tribe of the Middle Horde Photos: Luckert

[5]

3. *Khyz Khuwar*, a traditional game of horsemanship played between older boys and girls.

4. *Lakh Tartyw*, or *Kökpar Tartyw*, an all-male contest, played for the possession of a headless goat. Photos: Anonymous

[6]

5. Kazakh herder living at *Terekti Sai*, 60 km south of Urumqi. Photo: Luckert

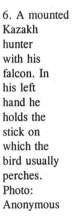

6. A mounted Kazakh hunter with his falcon. In his left hand he holds the stick on which the bird usually perches. Photo: Anonymous

7-8. A Kazakh cemetery, south of Urumqi. A Kazakk shaman in the Tarbaghatai Prefecture, singing. Photos: Luckert and Li Zengxiang.

[8]

9–10. A Kazakh shaman in the Tarbaghatai Prefecture, singing over a
mentally troubled woman who visited his home. Photos: Awelkhan Hali.

[9]

11. Zhamalkhan, a famous singer (akhyn), of Dörbezhin County, Tarbaghatai Prefecture, accompanied by an apprentice.

12. People on their way to a wedding ceremony. Photos: Anonymous

13. After the veil is removed from the bride's face, girls from the bridegroom's awyl come to visit their new sister-in-law.
Photo: Anonymous

14. A newly married lady, next to her bridal bed, wearing her bridal scarf. Photo: Luckert

15-16. A Kazakh lady at the Xinjiang College of Education. After their umbilical cord has dropped away, Kazakh infants sleep in a cradle until they are one year old. The mattress has a hole under the infant's buttocks, to keep it clean and dry. Photos: Anonymous

[12]

17-18. An opening at the top of the yurt is regulated for sunlight, fresh air, or for smoking meat. Prior to a meal, moments of silent prayer are concluded here with the words "Amen Allah!" Photos: Luckert

19-20. A family representing three generations poses for a photograph inside their yurt. Continuing to the right the older girls, self-consciously, line up by themselves. Photos: Luckert

[14]

21-22. Haystacks atop livestock sheds, and a school house nearby, indicate that this village in the *Terekti Sai* area, south of Urumqi, serves as a center for winter pasture. Photos: Luckert

[15]

23-24. Yurts nestled away in a valley edged with pine slopes. While younger men are with the herds, women and grand-parents watch their offspring. Photos: Luckert

[16]

25-26. Simple homesteads in the Ili region. This area is settled mostly by Albans and Khyzais who belong to the Great Horde. Photos: Witt

[17]

Chapter 1

From Waves of Tribes and Nations

This book on Kazakh traditions offers materials most of which were gathered among Kazakhs now living in northern Xinjiang, the Uighur Autonomous Region. It represents efforts at collecting folklore from the years prior to 1991. Henceforth, and in years to come, as cultural interchangés between Xinjiang and the Republic of Kazakhstan will become more frequent, efforts at collecting Kazakh traditions will surely be expanded—to embrace materials from all the Kazakh regions. Our book is being offered in anticipation, to stimulate more broadly based research efforts in the future.

Approximately seven million Kazakhs live now in Kazakhstan, in the new republic which in 1991 has gained full independence from Russia and the former Soviet Union. Kazakhs in the Peoples Republic of China represent one of the fifty-six nationalities (*minzu*). Their number in 1949 was recorded at 443,655; they were 847,997 strong in 1979. By 1982 they have grown to 907,582, and in 1985 they were 964,000. The 1989/90 Census gives their number at 1,111,718.

Most of the Chinese Kazakhs live in the Ili Kazakh Autonomous Prefecture, in the northern portion of the Tianshan Mountains. Some also live in the Tarbaghatai and the Altai prefectures.[1] The entire area is part of Xinjiang, the Uighur Autonomous Region. In addition, Kazakhs in China can be found in the Mulei (More) Kazakh Autonomous County of Changji, the Prefecture of the Hui Nationality, and in the Balikun (Barköl) Kazakh Autonomous County of the Hami (Khumul) Prefecture. A number of Kazakhs also live in the Mongol Autonomous County, Buertala (Bortala), in the city of Shihezi, and in Urumqi. Outside Xinjiang they can be found in the Akesai (Akhsai) Kazakh Autonomous County of the province of Gansu that borders on Xinjiang.

The Ili Prefecture is a beautiful region along Xinjiang's northern frontier, well endowed with natural resources. It covers 350,000 square kilometers—approximately one fifth of Xinjiang. The snowcapped Tianshan, Tarbaghatai, and Altai ranges are natural wonders to behold. The Ili, Ertis (Upper Irtysh), Ulenggur and Dörbilshin rivers, together with the Buwryltoghai, Khanas, and Sairam Lakes are jewels in Central Asian geography. Forests of mature trees extend upward along talus slopes. Fertile valleys provide oases with deep soils and rich pastures.

Legendary Origins

Two popular legends tell about the origins of the Kazakh people. Both are based on etymological speculation and are motivated by a desire to romanticize Kazakh origins. The first legend traces Kazakh origins to a common patriarch, whereas the second focuses on a leader acclaimed by several clans and tribes. Both legends are equally well known among all three Kazakh hordes *(zhüz)*, and both reflect socio-economic conditions that generally prevailed in Central Asia.

The "White Goose" Legend.—Long, long ago, there lived a chief who led a small clan; his name was Kharashaghadyr. He was a valiant warrior, showed great heroism, and was brave and skillful in battle. He often led armed men into battle against their enemies and all his people supported and loved him.

But on one occasion Kharashaghadyr suffered a defeat. His warriors were scattered in all directions and he himself was severely wounded. He dragged himself along, alone, in places devoid of human habitation. It was a hot summer day, and a scorching sun blazed mercilessly down onto his head. The Gobi desert was heating up all around him. Weakened by his deep wounds, tired and thirsty, he fell and lay there in the desert to breathe his last gasps.

Suddenly the sky broke open. A white female goose flew down toward Kharashagadhyr. A few drops of saliva dribbled from the beak of the goose into Kharashagadhyr's open mouth and ran down his throat. After that the goose brought him to the side of a blue lake. Kharashagadhyr drank some water and, little by little, his wounds healed and his strength returned. Then, in the twinkling of an eye the white goose turned into a beautiful young maiden. Kharashaghadyr and that young girl became husband and wife. Together they had a son. To memorialize their strange union they named their son "Kazakh" *(Khazakh)*—*khaz* means goose, and *akh* means white. Later this man Kazakh had three sons whom he named Bekarys, Akharys, and Zhanarys. The descendants of Bekaris formed the Great Horde; those of Akharys became the people of the Middle Horde; whereas the descendants of Zhanarys are known as the Small Horde.[2] In accordance with this legend the members of these three nomadic hordes all consider themselves to be descendants of the patriarch named "Kazakh."

The "Alash" Legend.—Long, long ago, in the Syr Darya river valley, lived a khan named Khyzylarystan (Red Lion). Thirty-two tribes were under his jurisdiction. Regularly he led the men of his tribes in punitive expeditions against other groups, and each time he captured many enemies. On one occasion he captured a beautiful girl whom he married. She bore him a son, and to his great astonishment the body of the child was covered with freckles. To decipher this omen Khyzylarystan resorted to divination, and the answer from the spirit world was auspicious. His concubine therefore advised him to throw the baby into the Syr Darya river. The khan accepted her advise and ordered his guards to do so.

By the river lived a poor old fisherman who saw the helpless baby floating downstream. He scooped it up, and he took the little boy home to his yurt. There he raised him as his own son. Because there were freckles all over the child's body the people took to calling him *"Alash"* (Piebald). Alash grew up and he was very clever and brave. He enjoyed the love and esteem of the people.

The khan Khyzylarystan later learned what had become of his son and he wanted to call him back. But his body guards, Khytanbai and Maghabai, disagreed. They suggested that Khyzylarystan give his son one hundred warriors as retinue and to let him roam carefree and in leisure. The khan Khyzylarystan agreed and ordered Khytanbai's oldest son, Üsün, to accompany Alash with one hundred horsemen. The next year the khan ordered Khytanbai's second son, Bolat, also to join Alash with one hundred horsemen. The third year the khan ordered Khytanbai's third son, Arshyn, also to accompany Alash with another one hundred horsemen. All these three hundred horsemen who accompanied Alash roamed freely, and they frequently raided neighboring clans and tribes to make them subservient. The people appropriately referred to these three hundred horsemen and to their subservient tribes as "Kazakhs," which means "brave and free men," or "carefree men of leisure."[3] Eventually these three hundred men elected Alash to be their khan, and so it came about that Alash ascended to the throne.

Alash divided his realm in three portions. The upper portion of the Syr Darya river valley was given to Üsün and his men, the middle portion to Bolat's group, and the lower valley to Arshyn and his people. In this manner these three areas have come to be occupied by the three Kazakh hordes. The Kazakh people consider themselves to be descendants of these three hundred freely roaming horsemen and therefore call themselves "Kazakh." They honor Alash as their first ruler.

Historical Origins

Ancient clans and tribes, some of which may have retained their identity from the 2nd century B.C.E. to the 15th century C.E., and which spoke Turkic dialects, eventually emerged as the Turkic group of nationalities we know today.[4] They spoke similar dialects which eventually emerged as the Turkic family of languages known today. These people bred and raised the same types of livestock, rode the same breeds of horses and fought with the same types of weapons. They shared the same social organization and overall culture. Moreover, inasmuch as the Kazakhs have been nomadic herders since times immemorial, they have had good socio-economic reasons to adhere to a patriarchal clan system. At the same time, with the influx of other tribes into the growing Kazakh confederation, pure patriarchal and patrilocal tradition could not always be maintained.

Fragments of that general Central Asian cultural and socio-economic configuration have splintered and were reunited many times, and in the 15th century such splinters have begun to come together to form the present-day Kazakh nationality.

The earliest inhabitants of western Central Asia were identified by Homer as the Cimmerians. They appeared in the southern steppe of Russia about twelve centuries B.C.E. Four hundred years later the Scythians appeared and began to eclipse Cimmerian culture. To the east of the Scythians, about two centuries B.C.E., Xiongnu (Hsiungnu) horsemen began haunting the western limits of China. Culturally in any case, the Xiongnu were continuous with the Scythians in the west. Their epicenter was Mongolia.

During the first century C.E. this first empire of nomads dissolved. Southern Xiongnu, in the Ordos region, submitted to China while some of their northern kinsmen eventually were absorbed by the Xianbei (Hsienpei) of Mongolia. Another remnant group of the Xiongnu, that was moving westward at the time, could have been the people who surfaced during the 4th century in southern Russia as the Huns.[5]

By the end of the 4th century the Juan-juan empire succeeded the Xiongnu and Xianbei in Mongolia. Then in 552 a Turk tribe, led by Bumin, usurped power from within the Juan-juan empire. His people held sway over Central Asia for the next two centuries. In 582 C.E. this Turkic kaghanate broke up into a western and an eastern portion. The western portion contained the area of present-day Xinjiang, the Pamirs, and most of Central Asia. East and west cooperated as far as they were motivated by common mercantile interests. Together the two regimes controlled the trade route between China and Byzantium, known as the Silk Road. They kept the caravans moving and profited by doing so.

The Chinese Tang took over Mongolia in 630. In 659 they extended their power to include Bukhara and Samarkand, in the west. But in 683 the Turkic empire reasserted itself in Mongolia and proceeded to hold in its reach all the lands that lay between China, Iran, India, and Byzantium. Turkic tribes occupied the Ili river valley and Semirechye (Seven rivers) area and maintained there a kaghanate between 698 and 700 C.E. Then the Karluks rose to power and prospered; they conquered the Turks and dominated the Ili river and Semirechye areas from 766 to 940 C.E.

Meanwhile, the Uighur empire which blossomed on the Mongolian steppes between 744 and 840 C.E. was a continuation of the preceding Turk hegemony. It featured a new set of rulers. This empire was overrun by the Kyrgyz (Kighiz) in 840 and, while the Uighur people fled to western Gansu and into the Turfan region of Xinjiang, this fallen empire continued to preserve its name and thereby lend it to the present-day Uighur nationality. After the "great migration" a number of Uighur kaghanates asserted themselves in the Gansu Corridor and in the Turfan area.[6] They were the Hexi Huihu (Uighur), the Gaochang Huihu (Uighur), and the Conglinxi (Western Pamirs) Huihu. By way of these kingdoms the Uighur name endured and over the centuries it continued to be transliterated into Chinese—although different characters were used for writing it. The name "Weiwuer," pronounced similar to present-day "Uighur," appears still in Ming records of the late 15th century.[7]

From 960 to 1211 C.E. ancient pre-Kazakh clans, who spoke a Turkic language, were under the rule of the Karakhanid empire that was established by Pamir Uighurs and other Turkic groups. During the 12th century these clans were subjected to the Kharakhytai (Karakitai) kaghanate which, in Chinese records, is mentioned as Western Liao (1124-1218 C.E.). From the 13th century to the 14th most of these peoples came under the rule of the Golden Horde; some were under the Chaghatai Horde. When, early during the 14th century the Golden Horde broke up, most of the clans that later became Kazakhs were for a time swept up into the White Horde. During the 15th century, in Central Asia, many clan alliances and hordes went in and out of existence. Proto-Kazakh clans were governed by, or became involved with, the White Horde in a variety of ways.

During the early 15th century the proto-Kazakh clans were distributed widely. The *Wusun* were in the Semirechye and Syr Darya valleys; the *Khangjü* lived in the middle and in the south of Kazakhstan, as well as near the foot of Kharataw Mountain along the lower end of the Zhetisuw river and along middle stretches of the Syr Darya. The *Kerei* moved about at Semirechye, along the Tarbaghatai Mountains, Ertis (Upper Irtysh) river, Zaysan Lake, and the Om and Tobol rivers. The *Naiman* roamed on pasture lands in the Isim river valley. Some *Khongyrat* people were living in central Kazakhstan, others along the lower ends of the Ertis, Syr Darya, and Zhetisuw rivers. The *Duwlat* could be found in the Ili river, Chu river, and Talas river valleys. The *Zhalajyr* were at the foot of Kharataw Mountain and in the Syr Darya river valley.

During the middle of the 15th century the Abul Khajyr kaghanate was established at the manor of the White Horde. Jungar Mongols invaded that kaghanate twice. They burned the settlements and devastated the region. In 1465 some 200,000 of Abul Khajyr's subjects migrated eastward to the Chu and Talas river valleys under the leadership of Zhanybek and Kerei, the two great-grandsons of Ulys-khan, the last khan of the White Horde. There the Mughul khan, Esen Bogha, settled them in the Chu and Talas river area. Subsequently they established there an independent Kazakh kaghanate. This may be regarded as the moment in Central Asian history when the Kazakh nationality, as we now know it, has come into being. A group of nomadic herders who spoke an Uzbek Turkic dialect, who pursued a nomadic culture and economy, have attracted others who joined them and added to their growth.[8] United the Kazakh clans and tribes could field an army of 200,000 horsemen, and this explains in part how they achieved hegemony over the entire steppe region of central Asia. Another reason for their growth is infusion of people from other tribes. So for example, pastoralists from among the Nogai, the Uzbek, and the Altai Mongols merged with Kazakhs and were absorbed.

The Great Horde inhabited the Semirechye region, the lands along the upper and middle portion of the Syr Darya and Ili rivers, and along the southern portion of Balkhash Lake. The Middle Horde, situated between the Great and the Small, occupied the Kharataw Mountains, Kökshetaw Mountains, and the northeastern portion of the Balkhash Lake area. It reached south as far as the Syr Darya river, and north into Siberia, into the grasslands surrounding Altai and Tarbaghatai, as well as the Ertis river region. People of the Small Horde roamed in the western portion of Kazakhstan, along the lower course of the Syr Darya river, around the Aral Sea, to the upper reaches of the Tobol river, and in areas between the Torghai and Erkhyzy rivers.

According to Hasakezu Wenhuashi, Kazakh tribes and clans were distributed among the three hordes in the following manner. The Üsün, Khangly, Duwlat, Zhalajyr, Alban and Suwan people were under the Great Horde. The Naiman, Kerei, Arghyn, Khypshak, Khongyrat, and Wakh belong to the Middle Horde. The Älimuly, Jetiuly, and Baiuly comprised the Small Horde.[9]

According to S. Baisheva, the Great Horde includes eleven tribes—Khangly, Sirgeli, Zhalajyr, Sary Uisin, Shanyshkhyly, Ysty, Shapyrashty, Oshakhty, Alban, Suwan, and Duwlat. To the Middle Horde belong Arghyn, Khypshakh, Naiman, Khongyrat, Kerei, Tarakhty, Wakh. To the Small Horde belong the tribes Älimuly, Baiuly, Zhetiruw.[10]

There has been considerable debate about when exactly the three Kazakh hordes came into being. According to some Chinese historical sources, and recent theories, the three hordes or *zhüz* were formed during the 16th century. Some scholars trace their origin even to the time of Khan Toqi of the Kazakh kaghanate (1698–1718).[11] The earliest traveler to identify these hordes was Tevkelev, the Russian envoy who was sent to the Small Horde in 1731.[12] Their existence was confirmed in 1734 by Kirillov, the leader of an expedition to Orenburg. The accounts of both men, as well as notations by the 18th century Russian travelers Rychkov and Georgii provide similar information about the size and location of these hordes. Vostrov and Mukanov, renowned scholars of Kazakh history, pinpoint the formation of the three hordes at the middle of the 16th Century, during the rule of Haq Nazar (1538-1580).[13] This appears to have been a time when the central authority of the kaghanate no longer could grasp and hold together the vast Kazakh geography. The kaghanate disintegrated into three distinct hordes.

Subsequent Kazakh history, and formative events in the Soviet Union and in China, are best left to specialized historians to sort out and to publish. Some of that information has been gathered and published in English by Benson/Svanberg and M.B. Olcott.[14] Their histories of the Kazakh presence in China, specifically, are being ignored by scholars who live in China—for a variety of reasons. The present volume on Kazakh traditions, which represents a joint effort by a Kazakh, a Chinese, and an American writer, need not stray beyond the bounds of the carefully delineated topic which made their cooperation possible in the first place.

The organization of the Kazakh nationality, as formerly it existed ideally within their kaghanate, may be reconstructed as a hierarchy of seven strata or layers.

1. At the bottom level is the settlement (*awyl*, aul), and people within these settlements may be interrelated in one of three ways: (a) there may be a clan or tribal affiliation; (b) there may be inter-

relatedness by marriage and bloodline; and finally (c) both "a" and "b" types of affiliation may exist together in a given *awyl*. The mixed type of settlement can be found most often where semi-agricultural and pastoral nomadic clans have come together. Usually five to ten families live in an *awyl*. Settlements have their own pastures. They are usually named after the *awyl bas*, the community's headman or chief. Most of the headmen are wealthy and experienced elders, and they assume responsibility for the welfare and safety of their people. They also are responsible for organizing marriages and funerals and for rendering help where needed. People within the entire *awyl* are expected to accept their chief's arrangements.

2. The next higher level is the *ata*. It is based on intermarriage among several settlements. People from settlements within the same *ata* may roam on each other's pasture lands. The headman of an *ata* is referred to as "White Beard" or "Venerable Elder" *(akhsakhal)*, and he is charged with the general affairs of his people. He mediates quarrels which arise between settlements.

3. A *ruw* (clan or tribe) may consist of fifteen *ata* or so. People of one *ruw* know themselves as descendants of the same ancestor, and the *ruw* is generally named after that common ancestor. Each *ruw* claims its traditional pasture lands and burial grounds. The headman of a *ruw* is the *ruwbasy*. All major affairs within the *ruw* should be under his jurisdiction.

4. Several *ruw* together make a *taipa*. The headman of a *taipa*, is called a *byj*. Traditionally these leaders were elected to arbitrate civil disputes, judge criminal cases, and resolve other major problems. Their function is to coordinate relations among the various *ruw*.

5. An *ulys* is an association of several *taipa* which reside in the same geographical area. The head of an *ulys* is referred to as a *sultan*. Only aristocrats (*akh süjek*, literally "white bones") could be elected to be sultans. Most of these were princes or sons of a king *(khan)*. The general population of Kazakh commoners was ranked as *khara süjek* (black bones).

6. A *zhüz* or horde, in ancient times, was a regional union of tribes or clans. Traditionally the Kazakh people were divided into three *zhüz*—into a Great, a Middle, and a Small horde. The head of a *zhüz* is a khan.

7. At the apex of a Kazakh horde traditionally was enthroned a king or *khan*. A khan who had aspirations to command the remaining

Kazakh hordes as well was also known as *khaghan*. He was the highest authority in the traditional Kazakh social and political order.

Tributary Clans, Tribes, and Confederations

Much of the history of various Kazakh clans and tribes, of clan associations and tribal confederations, can still be traced in Chinese and other historical records. Their history can to some extent also be reconstructed from Kazakh pedigrees that are being handed down orally. The Kazakh nation has retained to this day its clan-and-tribe-based political structure. In a reconstruction of the Kazakh historical identity all these sociological factors must therefore be taken into consideration.

According to the combined opinion of Kazakh, Chinese, as well as foreign scholars, the clans and tribes that contributed to the Kazakh confederation included Saks, Indo-Scythes, Wusun, Kang Ju (Sogdians), Alani, Xiongnu (Huns), and other ancient groups that lived and roamed in Central Asia.

The Saks—Before 200 B.C.E. Sak people lived in Central Asia. The *Xi Yu* biography, from the Han dynasty, tells that "there are Saks and Indo-Scythes among the Wusun."[15] The Chinese historian and geographer Xu Song (1781-1848) wrote that "Sak was the name of a state in Central Asia."[16]

Greek historians mentioned a confusing array of tribal names that were current among the Saks. They are Masaget, Jaksart, Abyi, Dahyi or Dai, Kharat, Komar, Askhatagh, Jissedon or Assyi, Aryimassyp, Sarmat, Kaspyi, and more. The Masaget and Jaksart lived south and northeast of the Aral Sea, also south of the Syr Darya river. The Dahyi dwelt in the lower valley of the Syr Darya and in the hinterland of the Aral Sea. The Abyi tribe was scattered among the Tianshan mountains and along the central region of the Syr Darya river. The Kharat tribe roamed northeast and northwest of the Kharataw and Alataw mountains, along the Talas river, while the Komar tribe lived in the valleys of the Keles, Shyrshykh, and Angiren rivers. The Askhatagh people were spread over the central Alataw Mountains and the grasslands of the Chu and Talas rivers. The Jissedon and Assyi tribes moved between the Ili and the Chu rivers and into the Tarbaghatai Mountains. The Aryimassyp people lived north and northeast of the Jissedon people, along the western slopes of the Altai mountains. The Sarmat people settled on the opposite side of the Caspian Sea, east to the Zhem river and north to the source of the Zhajykh river. The Kaspyi people lived east of the Black Sea; they have lend their name, on our maps, to the "Caspian Sea."[17] Most of the people in these areas today consider themselves to be Kazakhs. It seems probable, therefore, that the ancient Saks contributed their lineages to the formation of the present-day Kazakh nationality.

The Indo-Scythes (Chin. "Rouzhi," Kaz/Chin. "Jozi")—During the time of the Qin Dynasty (221–206 B.C.E.), and of the Han (206 B.C.E.–220 C.E.), people of the Indo-Scythian tribal confederation moved about in search of pasture among the Dun Huang and the Qilian mountains. Indo-Scythes formed one of the largest states West of the Xiongnu. "The Indo-Scythes were nomadic tribes that moved about with their livestock; their customs were identical with those of the Xiongnu (Huns)."[18] Xu Song explained: "The color of the Indo-Scythes was white and reddish; they were good at horseback riding and arrow shooting."[19] Kang Tai sums up what he knows concerning numbers, and about the world, by way of quoting anonymous foreigners: "Foreigners say that there are three things which are plentiful (in this world), in China it is population, in the Roman Empire it was treasures, and among the Indo-Scythes it was horses."[20]

In 209 B.C.E. the man Mo Du made himself the chief of the Xiongnu. He then attacked Dong Hu in the east, and in the west he pushed through the Indo-Scythes. After Mo Du's death, in 174 B.C.E., his son Ji Zhou (?–161 B.C.E) succeeded him. Ji Zhou killed the chief of the Indo-Scythes, and from his skull he made a drinking bowl for himself. At that time the political power of the Indo-Scythes collapsed completely. Under pressure and attacks from the Xiongnu, Indo-Scythian tribes then moved into the valleys of the Ili region.

From the "Biography of Zhang Qian," in the *Han Shu*, we read: "The Indo-Scythes were defeated by the Xiongnu; they moved westward to attack the Saks who in turn, while the Indo-Scythes lived on their lands, moved far to the south."[21] Historians believe that this happened between 174 and 160 B.C.E.

The Wusun—Some Chinese scholars think that the Wusun are the same people who later surfaced as the Üsün (Üsin), and therefore are one of the primary groups that merged to form the present-day Kazakh nationality. According to Kazakh historical legends and pedigree, "Üsün" in the narrow sense represents the name of a tribe that belongs to the Great Horde. In the broader sense it refers to tribes that inhabit the Ili river valley, the Zheti Suw River valley, and southern Kazakhstan. The present-day tribes of Alban, Suwan, and Zhalajyr have become separated from the Üsün. Shokhan Välikhanov informs us that "Üsün was the ancestor of the entire Great Horde."[22]

The ancient tribe of Wusun rose abruptly when, in 160 B.C.E., they put together a strong political organization. The earliest Chinese historical records to mention the Wusun are the "Biographies of Farghana" in the *Shi Ji*, and the "Biographies of Xi Yü" in the *Han Shu*. There we learn that the Wusun, before they moved west into the Ili river valley, roamed as nomads between Daxata (Dun Huang) and the Qilian Mountains, that is, in a small area west of the Xiongnu.[23] According to *Han Shu Wusun Zhuan* (*Wusun Biography in the History of the Han Dynasty*), the population of the Wusun at their height reached 630,000; there were approximately 120,000 families; Nandoumi was their leader.[24]

The Wusun were attacked by one of its powerful neighbors, and families were broken up. Some fled, some died, and some went into exile. Who was this powerful neighbor? The *Shi Ji* and the *Han Shu* give different answers. According to the *Shi Ji*, "Xiongnu attacked the Nandoumi and conquered their realm." According to the *Han Shu*, "Indo-Scythes attacked the Nandoumi and captured their lands."

The Kangju—These people maintained their ancient state between Lake Balkhash and the Aral Sea. East of the Kangju state lived the Wusun, the Yan Cai west of them, and Indo-Scythes occupied the land to the south. The Kangju spoke a Turkic language.

Kangju people are first mentioned in "Biographies of Farghana" in the *Shi Ji*, then in the *Jin Shu* (*History of the Jin Dynasty*). Some historians think that in the *Mongqol-un Nihuca Tobciyan* (*Secret History of Yuan*) the tribal name of Kangju is given as Kang-li, identical with the name of the Khangly tribe that belongs to the present-day Kazakh nationality. According to the *Shi Ji* the domain of the Kangju was north of Farghana.

In European records the Kangju or Khangly are identified as Sogdians.[25] According to Kazakh historical legends and pedigrees, in ancient times the Kangju people lived in the Syr Darya river valley. These Kangju were divided into Khara Kangju (Black Kangju), and Sary Kangju (Yellow Kangju). This tradition agrees with the "Biographies of Farghana" in the *Shi Ji*. During the Han Dynasty (206 B.C.E. to 220 C.E.) Kangju became a large state, and their population reached 600,000. There were approximately 120,000 families and a similar number of soldiers. Kangju remained a large state from 220 to 581 B.C.E.[26] Later generations of their people mixed with Kazakhs, Karakalpaks, and Uzbeks.[27]

The Alani—Some historians regard the Alani, who are mentioned in Chinese historical records around 200 B.C.E. as the ancestors of the Alchin people, a tribe or tribal confederation that now belongs to the Small Horde. Another Chinese name of the Alani is Yan Cai.[28] According to *Biographies of Xi Yu*, in the *Hou Han Shu*, the name of the state of Yan Cai was changed to Alanlias. But Nyjhmet Myngzhan, a Chinese Kazakh scholar, thinks that Yan Cai and Alani, or Alanliao, are not different spellings of the name of a state; they are perhaps the names of related but distinct tribes that inhabited the same area. While the Yan Cai were powerful and prosperous, the Alani were weaker and submitted to Yan Cai rule. As a result of this integration both tribes together became known as "Alani." Ancient historical records did not distinguish between Yan Cai and Alani and simply referred to them as a union of clans.[29]

According to Chinese historical records, Yan Cai and Alani were spread over a large area around the Aral Sea. During Han times they were nomads who also engaged in agriculture. Their customs and their attire were the same as those of the Kangjü.

The Xiongnu—The Xiongnu are an ancient nationality which in Chinese is also known as Hu. In Kazakh language they are identified as Hunder. The suffix "-der" signifies the plural form of "Hun." The Huns rose to power approximately 200 years before the Common Era. They were dislodged in the east three hundred years later. At the time of their chief, Mo Du (?–174 B.C.E.) they defeated many tribes around them and controlled an area that stretched east to the Liao river, west to the Congling Mountains (Pamirs), to Lake Baikal, and south to the Great Wall. From historical records we know that some Xiongnu mingled and blended with what became the Kazakh nationality.[30]

From Kazakh inscriptions and sayings we can infer a connection that might have existed between Kazakh and Xiongnu people. For example, an epiphet of the ancient Khypshakh—a designation still given to a present-day Khypshakh tribe—was "Oibas and Ojyrbas." Oibas is the name of a Xiongnu hero. It is on this basis that many scholars have concluded that the Khypshakh are descendants of the Xiongnu.[31]

*   *   *

Some ancient proto-Kazakh clans and tribes came under the rule of the Western Turkish kaghanate (567–659 C.E.), under the Türkesh kaghanate (698–766 C.E.), under the Karluk kaghanate (766–940 C.E.), under the Karakhanid dynasty (940–1213 C.E.) and under the Karakitai or Western Liao empire (1130–1218 C.E.). Here follow the names of some of the ancient tribes that emerged into the full light of history:

The Khasa—The name of one of the Turkish tribes, Khasa, was also written "Hesa," "Asa," or "Khasar." They were descendants of the Yan Cai from the time of the Han dynasty.

The Khasa are not very well documented in Chinese historical records. But we know that Khasa people lived west of the Western Turkic kaghanate, far away from their political center. The *Jiu Tang Shu* and the *Xin Tang Shu* indirectly mention their geographical location.[32] South of them were the Parsa, the Sham, and the Constantinopolitans, and southeast were the Khwari.[33]

There are some mentionings of the Khasa in the Persian book *Hudud al-Ghalam*: "East of Khasa between the sea and the mountains is the Great Wall. Their southern portion is Saler (Salar, Salor, Salur), and to the west are huge mountains. This is a very beautiful and richly endowed realm. They have many cows and sheep and they trade slaves.... Their capital, and the city in which their khan lives is Etil. Turks give the name of Volga to Etil. Their khan was titled targhan, and their armies are stationed in the western part of Etil City.... In the other portion of the city live the Muslims and the idolaters. The khazar (khan) has seven officials, and these seven officials subscribe to seven different religions."[34] From such statements it is possible to infer that the seven officials might have been the heads of seven different tribes.

The Duwlat—In ancient times the name of the present-day Duwlat tribe, which belongs to the Great Horde, was in various languages written Dawlu, Duwli, Duwlugh, Daluw, Duwlyghas, Dalugh, or Doghlat. In his book, *Problems in Kazakh Linguistic History and Dialects*, the Soviet Kazakh scholar S. A. Amanzholov observed that "where Chinese historians wrote Duwlu, Persians wrote Dughlat or Dukulat."[35]

According to Chinese historical records, the Duwlu union of clans belonged to the Western Turkic kaghanate.[36] The Duwlu had five clans, and each clan had its own chief. The chief's official title was "Chuo," which signifies that the largest clan of the Duwlu union was Turkic, and it spread from the Ili river to the Chu river valley. Khoilaw, the second largest clan, spread from the Barlykh Mountains to the vicinity of Lake Ebinor. Shyimojyn, the third clan, was in the Tarbaghatai Mountains, and Zhanys, the fourth, spread in the Big Star (*Ülken Zhuldyz*) and the Little Star (*Kishi Zhuldyz*) region. Finally, Isti, the smallest of the Duwlu clans was found east of the Ili river and in the Buratala region.[37]

From a variety of historical records similar conclusions may be drawn: before the Common Era the Duwlat were included among the Wusun.[38] Along this line, Duwlat history blends into Kazakh history.

Nüshbe—According to Chinese historical records, the *Jiu Tang Shu* and the *Xin Tang Shu*, the Nüshbe union included five clans. All of these clans belong to the right (south) portion of the Western Turkic kaghanate. They are: (1) Azghyz Kül Erkin; (2) Khaso Kül Erkin; (3) Baryskhan Ton Ashbar Erkin; (4) Azghyz Nyizhukh Erkin; (5) Khaso Shopan Erkin.[39] Azghyz, Khaso, and Baryskhan are clan names. Kül, Ton Ashbar, Nyizhukh, and Shopan are the names of famous Nüshbe chiefs. Erkin is the official title of the chief, and ulus means clan.

The clan confederations of Khasa, Duwlat, and Nüshbe were formed under the rule of the Western Turkic kaghanate.

Türkesh—The Türkesh clan was one of the five clans of the Duwlat tribe, of the Western Turkic kaghanate. After 659 C.E., while that kaghanate was being destroyed by the Tang dynasty, the Türkesh clan developed rapidly and build up its own kaghanate between the Ili river and Chu river basins, an area which formerly was under the

Western Turkic kaghanate. The Türkesh people were divided into two groups, the Yellow family and the Black family. Each family had its own chief, and they disputed among themselves until the fortunes of the clan declined. After 766-779 C.E. they submitted to the rule of the Karluk.

The Karluk—In antiquity the Karluk were a nomadic Turkic-speaking people who lived in the Altai and Tarbaghatai mountains. They, too, contributed to the formation of the Kazakh nationality. Their tribal union included three clans: Bolat, Zhüz, and Tashly. After the middle of the 8th Century the Türkesh in the area were waning. Karluk clans occupied the lands and established their own kaghanate. Eventually all the Türkesh people came under their rule. Later, during the first years of the Northern Song Dynasty (960-1127 C.E.), Karluks built up the Karakhanid dynasty together with some Uighurs and Yagmas. Some scholars regard the Arghyn clan, in the Middle Horde, to have descended from the Bolat, a clan that was ruled by Karluks.

The Khyimakh—The name "Khyimakh" often appears in Arabic and Persian historical sources during the Middle Ages. In the Dictionary of Turkic Languages *(Divanü Lughat—at Türk)*, compiled by Mahmud Kashgari during the 11th Century, Khyimakh was written "Yemäk." In Chinese historical records the Khyimakh are not mentioned.

During the 7th Century the Khyimakhs lived in the Ertis river valley and north of the Altai Mountains. At that time they were under the rule of the Western Turkic kaghanate. After that kaghanate collapsed in 656 C.E., they took possession of the middle portion of the Ertis river by force, during the 8th Century. Little by little they expanded their territory westward. During the 9th Century they occupied the land as far as Alaköl Lake, northwest of the Zhetisuw river. Balkhash Lake was the boundary between the Khyimakhs and the Karluks. Later, during the second half of the 9th Century, the Khyimakh kaghanate was founded.

According to the Persian book on geography, *Hudud äl-ghalam*, Kirghiz people lived east of the Khyimakh, and along the Khyimakh's boundary flowed the Ertis and Syr Darya rivers. To their west lived the Khypshakhs, whereas the north was desolate and uninhabited.[40]

During the 11th Century the Khyimakh kaghanate disintegrated. The Khypshakhs intruded and occupied their lands. Khyimakh people came under the rule of the Khypshakh clan union.

The Kharahanyi—By the middle of the 10th Century the Kharahanyi expanded their kaghanate into a fullfledged empire. During the 12th Century they were in decline. Nevertheless, at the height of their power and prosperity they occupied lands between the Amu Darya river, included most of Central Asia as far as the southern oases of the Tarim Basin.[41] Uighur, Karluk, Jaghma, Oghyz, and Chyghyl—including Üsin, Khangly, Duwlat, Teli, Khyrghyz (Kirghiz), Khypshakh, Arghyn and Oghyz which eventually emerged together as the Kazakh nationality—were the primary tribes and clan unions that comprised the Kharahanyi empire.

During the end of the 10th Century the Kharahanyi empire split into two portions, western and eastern. After the split numerous conflicts flared up between the ruling khans and erupted into one war after another. As a result the empire declined until Yeludashi (1087-1143 C.E.) led his Karakitai army to conquer Balsagun and the Kharahanyi empire in 1134 C.E.

Though shortlived by itself, the Kharahanyi empire was instrumental in permanently changing the religious landscape of Central Asia. The Kharahanyi domain was the first Turkic realm that converted to the religion of Islam. Early in the 10th Century C.E. the khan Satuq Bughra became a Muslim; his Islamic name was Khan Abdal Kerim. During the reign of this son, Musa bin Abdal Kerim, the whole empire was converted to the way of Islam by the dedicated labors of Sufi missionaries.

Kharakhytai—In Chinese records "Kharakhytai" (Karakitai) is known as Western Liao; it was established as a dynasty around 1130/1131 C.E. and lasted a decade or so into the next century. While the aristocrats of Khytai (of the Liao Dynasty) moved westward to Xiyü and occupied more of Central Asia, one of the Khytai nobles at Kerman, present-day Samarkand, made himself king and named his state Kharakhytai. The territory extended in the southeast to the Amu Darya river, to Balkhash Lake in the northwest, and east as far as present-day Xinjiang. Thus, during that period all the peoples who later came to constitute the Kazakh nationality fell under the jurisdiction of the Khytai rulers. In 1212 C.E. the Naiman people moved westward and intruded into Kharakhytai territory. They terminated the leadership of Zhilugur who was the last khan of the Kharakhytai, but they retained the name "Kharakhytai" to designate their own state. In 1218 Kharakhytai was conquered by the Mongols.

The Rise of the Mongols

During the 13th century the Mongols rose to power and began moving like an avalanche. Under its most renowned leader, Chingis Khan, the Mongol kaghanate shook the world. Early during the 13th century the Mongols conquered Tatar, Khongyrat, Zhalajyr, Oirat, Kerei, Merkit, Naiman, Wakh, and many other groups. Inasmuch as the Mongolian avalanche rolled over China as well, and established there the Yuan Dynasty, the names of many old clans who later combined to form the Kazakh nationality can be found in Chinese historical records. We shall introduce them individually:

Kerei—Before the Mongols rose to power the Kerei were prominent. Kerei is one of the largest tribes belonging to the Middle Horde in the Altai region. Historical records from the Middle Ages, such as *Mongqol-un Nihuca Tobciyan* (*The Secret History of the Mongols*), and *History of the Yuan Dynasty*, indicate that in those times the name Kerei was written in its plural form as Kereyit.

The Persian historian, Rashid al-Din Fadl Allah (1247-1318), explains in his book *Jami al-Tawarikh*: "It is alleged that in ancient time there lived a monarch who had seven sons. The skin color of every one turned out to be dark. That is the reason why they were called Kereyit. Later the descendants of these sons were given different names for their lineages. 'Kereyit' was the name of the branch headed by a monarch named Kereyit, while other branches without monarchs became subjects of the Kereyit."[42]

The Kazakh word "Ker" has two meanings; one is "light chestnut color," and the other is "superciliously arrogant." Information concerning this matter can also be found in Abilghazi al-Horezmi's *Turkic Pedigree*: "Because the facial color of the seven brothers was chestnut brown, their descendants were named Kereyit, and they came from the Oghyz (Oghuz) clan."[43]

From 907 to 1234 C.E., during the Liao and Jin dynasties, the Kerei were fragmented into small clans that moved about in the Orkhon and Jola river valleys; these were Kereihan, Jerhan, Tonhayit, Shiyat, Tobawut, and Albat.[44] About their social stratification is known that upper-class elements subscribed to the Nestorian Christian religion.[45]

According to Kazakh pedigree records, the Kerei consist of three tribes; Kharakerei, Sarykerei, and Wakhkerei. However, in modern times Kharakerei, one of the most powerful clan associations, has joined the Naiman confederation, and Wakhkerei or Wakh has become an independent tribe.

The Kerei clan union of the Kazakh nationality, which presently exists in Xinjiang, consists of twelve clans. These are Zhädik, Zhäntekei, Sheriwshi, Kharakhas, Molkhy, Könsadakh, Ijteli, Shybaraighyr, Zhastaban, Sarbas, Merkit, and Shyimojyn.

Naiman—This group has been mentioned earlier as an old clan comprised of Turkic speaking people. It is now one of the largest confederations of clans within the Middle Horde. In territories under Chinese jurisdiction the Naiman people can be found in the Altai, Tarbaghatai and Ili regions, thus, in the northern part of Xinjiang.

The Naiman have a long history. In the days of the Liao and Jin dynasties (until 1234 C.E.) they were nomads who moved about in search of pasture, as were other Turkic speaking peoples. Their primary areas were the Altai mountains, the Kharakhurum mountains, possibly also Alwi-Sraas, and the Kök Ertis mountains with the Ertis river bottom land. Their neighbors were Kirghiz and Uighurs.[46] In 1206 C.E. the Mongolian Chingis Khan attacked the Naiman and Merkit. He killed the Naiman chief and occupied their territories. Naiman people fled in all directions, and a number of them reached the Imil basin and Beshbalykh. There they blended in with the Kazakhs.

Under the rule of Tajan khan (?-1204) the Naiman people were known as Nestorian Christians.[47] However, when Tajan's son Küshlik married Hunhuwgha, the daughter of khan Jiyluwguw (who died in 1213 C.E.), he converted to Buddhism and pursued an intolerant policy toward Islam. Most of the people who lived in territories governed by the Western Liao dynasty happened to be Muslims. Küshlik compelled these people to embrace Buddhism or Nestorianism.[48]

There are today on record four variant traditions of Naiman pedigree. These are most easily shown by way of diagrams. Differences among these three traditions are best explained by the fact that different informants, from different lineages, might know their own pedigrees better than those of others.[49]

VARIANT ONE:

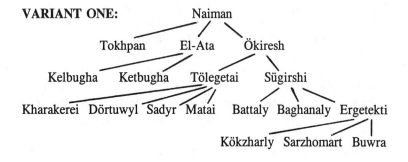

VARIANT TWO:

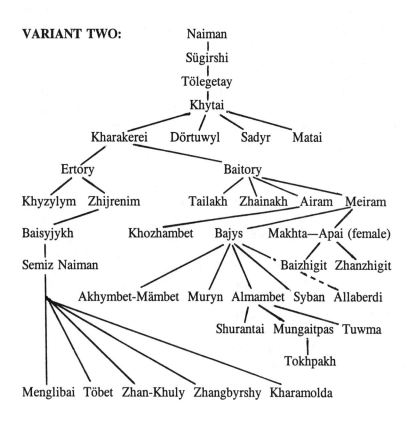

VARIANT THREE:

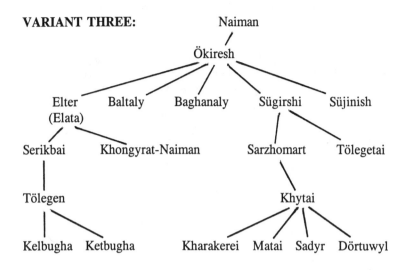

VARIANT FOUR:

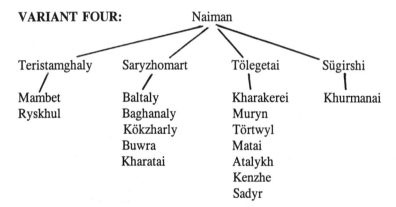

The Saryzhomart lineage—
Baltaly: Mardan, Begis
Baghanaly: Aktaz, Khyzyltaz, Shegedik, Shegelik, Khokhan, Zhyrykh,
       Zhurtshy, Ijbeske, Bainazar, Sarghaldakh
Kökzharly: Alystym, Khara, Esenäli, Zhärke, Kharshygha
          (Alystym: Üizhyghar, Ijtbakhbas)
          (Esenäli: Angdaghul, Khoisary)
Buwra: Shege, Alywshy, Syrdakh, Khangly, Ümbetkhul, Sultankhul, Zharas,
       Khuttuwdy

Kharatai: Boranshy, Tongmuryn, Beiseke, Shongmuryn, Khozhas, Khozhamberdi, Däwlet, Sheriwshi, Teneke, Shyimojyn, Sarghaldakh

The Tölegetai lineage—
Kharakerei: Mämbetkhul, Syban, Bolatshy, Tuwma, Baighana, Tokhpakh, Sary, Khozhambet, Akhymbet, Ersary, Khyrzhy, Zhastaban, Shürentai, Semiz-naiman, Akhnaiman, Tailakh, Zhainakh, Balkhabet
Muryn: Baizhigit
       (Baizhigit: Zhumykh, Toghas, Mämbet)
Törtwyl
Matai: Khaptaghai
       (Khaptaghai: Khydyräli, Khulshan, Törtkhara, Tolybai, Törtsary, Akhtiles, Köldei, Zhumai, Kharzhaw, Börte
Atalykh: Shaghyr
       (Shaghyr: Derbis, Begimbet, Ijtelmen, Mengis)
       [Derbis: Däwish, Alpysbai]
       [Begimbet: Sasan, Hasen, Shatan, Khastei]
       [Mengis: Alty]
Kenzhe: Sakhai, Elkhondy, Zhasykh, Yndysh, Saibolat, Khudas, Tybysh, Khoikel, Tiles
Sadyr: Ton, Shüje, Saryzhetim, Esenkhul, Tügelbai

Merkit—Nowadays the Merkit people are one of the twelve clans of the Kerei clan union, and as such they belong to the Middle Horde. Most Merkits in China are living in the Jemenei county of the Altai region.

During the Liao (907–1125 C.E.) and Jin (1115–1234 C.E.) dynasties, Merkit was a large, independent, and powerful tribe. The Selenga river basin was their homeland. North of them lived the Kirghiz, Khomat, and Oirat tribes. South of them were the Kerei. In the east they touched on the Naiman, and Mongols lived in the west. During a battle with the Mongols east of the Aral Sea, most of the Merkits were subdued by Mongolian troops of Chingis Khan's second son Juchi. A portion of the Merkits moved south and combined with Kerei. Among those Merkits were small clans like Lepes, Shaghyr, Almymbet, and Khulsary. Most Merkits continued to adhere to their tribal shamanistic religion, while some of them were Nestorians.[50]

Khongyrat—Nowadays the Khongyrat constitute a large clan that belongs to the Middle Horde. Yet, during the Liao and Jin dynasties they lived as nomads on the Mongolian Plateau, in parts of the Kerewlin and Erguna river valleys. Along their western flank were the

Mongols, and southwest of them grazed the herds of Tatars. The name Khongyrat first appears in the *History of the Liao Dynasty.* In the course of time some of the Khongyrat people blended in with the Mongols, and others mixed with the Kazakh nationality.

On the lips of Kazakh people who live in the area are many epic poems about heroism and love—and the famous Kazakh hero Alpamys Batyr came from the Khongyrat clan.[51]

"Muhabbat Name" (the Muhabbat Name epic) is such famous epic.[52] Its author, Muhammad Horezmi, came from the Khongyrat clan as well. His poem is written in the Khongyrat dialect that was used around 1353 C.E. by Kazakhs, Uzbeks, and other Turkic-speaking tribes that lived on the Khypshakh grasslands.

Zhalajyr—Nowadays the Zhalajyr belong to the Great Horde. According to the *Jami al-Tawarikh*, the Zhalajyr had a large population and were widely dispersed over the Mongolian Plateau. When Chingis Khan rose to power the Zhalajyr submitted to his rule, and when Chingis Khan went on his campaign toward Iran, his army included Zhalajyr soldiers, officers, and generals.[53] Zhalajyr people who remained in Central Asia were absorbed into the Kazakh nationality. According to Kazakh pedigrees, the Zhalajyr were divided into two large clans, the Shumanakh and Syrmanakh.

During the 15th and 16th centuries some Zhalajyrs were living in Siberia. Khydyrghaly Khosyn-uly Zhalajyry—from his name we know he was of the Zhalajyr tribe—wrote a book titled *Zhylnamalar zhyjnaghy,* an Almanac. He was a nephew of the khan Tokhy, a teacher and advisor of the Kazakh sultan Oraz Muhammad. His book tells about events in Kazakh lands from the 13th to the 16th centuries; he recorded pedigrees of khans, sultans, and bijs. In the process he also gave us a sketch of his life.[54]

Khypshakh—Historians have concluded that the Khypshakh are another ancient tribal confederation that has merged with others to form the Kazakh nationality. In fact, the Khypshakhs contributed heavily to its present composition and to the formation of its common language. The Khypshakh first appeared in Chinese historical records during the Han dynasty (206 B.C.E.–220 C.E.). They are as ancient as the Wusun and the Kangjü.

Until the early 13th Century the Khypshakh were powerful and prosperous. They ranged from the Ertis to the Volga, and they moved about in search of pasture between the Aral Sea and the Black Sea. The entire region came to be called the Khypshakh Grasslands. Everyone living in this realm was therefore counted as a Khypshakh. In Turkic, Mongolian, and Persian sources these people were referred to as Khypshakh, Kipshak, and Kifshak. In early Chinese sources they are Kefucha, Qibuchawu, or Gubishao—Qincha during the Middle Ages. In European languages they are Quman, and the Russians knew them as Polovtsi.

According to records from the 11th to the 13th Century, the Khypshakh people were divided into two groups. The Volga was the boundary they shared between them. To the east of the Volga lived the "Eastern Khypshakh" and west of that river the "Western Khypshakh." It was mostly easterners who later merged with the Kazakhs. The Khypshakh confederation of clans is now counted with the Middle Horde. Of course, other Khypshakh people have blended in with the Kirghiz, the Qaraqalpaks, Uzbeks, and Tatars.

In early times the Khypshakh people practiced a shamanistic religion. They revered Heaven, Earth, Water, Fire, and more. Before Islam spread to the Khypshakh grasslands, during the 12th Century, Christianity had a presence in that area.[55] Tribal shamanistic ways have endured especially among nomadic pastoralists who in large numbers roam at considerable distance from missionaries, mullahs, and mosques.

Notes

1. The Ili Kazakh Autonomous Prefecture is a "provincial" prefecture; it actually governs three prefectures—Ili, Tarbaghatai, and Altai.

2. In Turkic languages *zhüz* means part, division, side, or a hundred. The three Kazakh *zhüz* are explained as "hordes" of semi-nomadic kindred people who became separated by geography. See Anonymous, *Ci Hai* (*Book of Nationalities*), Shanghai: Dictionary Publishing House, 1978. However, the fact that a Kazakh *zhüz* or "horde" is in practice delineated as a numerical entity does sug-

gest—what histories of constituent clans confirm—that consanguinity probably was not the most consistent element in the original ethnic Kazakh configuration.

3. T. Zhanbolatov, a Kazakh scholar in the former Soviet province of Kazakhstan, explains that *khaz* means a very brave man, a hero, someone free and independent; *akh* is the ancient plural suffix. See *Zhuldyz* (*Star Journal*) 3, 1983. However, M.B. Olcott, in *The Kazakhs*. Stanford: Hoover Institution Press, 1987, pp. 3-27, follows Chokan Valikhanov and derives *kaz* from the Turkic verb *qaz* (to wander). Accordingly, these freely roaming men may from an outsider's perspective be classified, kindly as "nomads," and not so kindly as "vagabonds."

4. It is not a realistic aspiration for this team of international co-authors, who have agreed to collaborate in the humble task of informing the English-speaking world about a few Kazakh traditions in China, to also occupy themselves thoroughly with the knotty problems of Kazakh history and historio-graphy. Until more analytical historical works are forthcoming, from scholars inside China and elsewhere in the world, we offer this sketchy introduction merely as a "warming up" to Kazakh traditions. Meanwhile we refer our English readers to the tentative histories in Linda Benson & Ingvar Svanberg, *The Kazakhs of China, Essays on an Ethnic Minority*. Uppsala: Acta Universita-tis Upsaliensis, 1988; and in M.B. Olcott, *The Khazakhs*. Stanford: Hoover Institution Press, 1987.

5. "The Countries of Central Asia, the Region." *Encyclopedia Brittanica*, vol. 15., 15th ed., 1995, 702–714.

6. See Kwanten, Luc. *Imperial Nomads*. Philadelphia: University of Pennsylvania Press, 1979, pp. 52–53.

7. For details see Cuiyi Wei and Karl W. Luckert, *Uighur Stories from Along the Silk Road*, a book forthcoming.

8. Precise dating of the first Kazakh khanate is difficult because none of the contemporary accounts of the late fifteenth century paid much attention to the steppes. See Martha Brill Olcott, *The Kazakhs* (Stanford: Hoover Institution Press, 1987), p. 8.

9. See Su Beihai, ed. *Hasakezu Wenhuashi* (*A Cultural History of the Kazakh Nationality*). Urumqi: Xinjiang University Press, 1989, pp. 33-34.

10. S. Baisheva, editor. *Shezhire—Khazakhtyng Ruw-Taipalykh Khurylysy* (*Pedigree Structure of Kazakh Clans and Tribes*). Alma-Ata: Rawan Publishing House, 1991, pages 11, 21, 33.

11. See Chen Yongling, ed. *Dictionary of Nationalities*, Shanghai: Dictionary Press, 1987, p. 215.

12. In 1731 the chief khan of the Small Zhüz sent a delegation to Russia requesting to become a subject of Russia in defense against the Jungars. Peter the First sent Aleksei Ivanovich Tevkelev on a two year long diplomatic mission to Kazakhstan (1731–1733). In his diary Tevkelev wrote about the social structure and history of the Kazakh people.

13. See Olcott, *The Kazakhs*, p. 10. See also "The Countries of Central Asia—the Region." *Encyclopedia Brittanica*, vol. 15., 15th ed., 1995, 702–714.

14. See Benson and Svanberg above, in note 4, and M.B. Olcott, *The Kazakhs* (Stanford, 1987), pp. 124-126, 149, 170, 185. Compare also "The Countries of Central Asia, the Region," *Encyclopedia Brittanica*, vol. 15, 15th ed., 1995, pp. 702–714.

15. See Ban Gu concerning "Men of the Eastern Han Dynasty," in *Han Shu* (*History of the Han Dynasty*) 96:2, p. 3901. Beijing: Zhonghua Publishing House, 1962.

16. See Jian Bozan et al. *Lidai Gezu Zhuanji Huibian* (*Compilations of Biographies among Nationalities in Past Dynasties*), Beijing: Zhonghua Publishing House, 1957, p. 365, note 11. Xu Song is known for his linguistic research of geographical names. He was a specialist of Xinjiang history and geography. His major works are *Xiyu Shui-dao Ji* (*Records of Water Courses of Xiyu*), and *Han Shu Xiyu Zhuan Bu Zhu* (*Additional Notes on the Xiyu Biography of Han Shu*).

17. *Hasakezu Jian Shi* (*A Brief History of the Kazakh Nationality*). Urumqi: People's Publishing House of Xinjiang, 1987, pp. 32-33.

18. Sima Qian. *Shi Ji—Dawan Lie Zhuan* (*Biographies of Far-ghana*), 2nd edition, Volume 10, p. 3161. Beijing: Zhonghua Publishing House, 1982.

19. See Jian Bozan et al. *Lidai Gezu Zhuanji Huibian* (Compilation of Biographies among Nationalities in Past Dynasties), Beijing: Zhonghua Publishing House, 1957, p. 381, note 4.

20. Kang Tai. His book, *Biographies of Foreign States During the Wu Period*, is cited in Jian Bozan et. al. *Lidai Gezu Zhuanji Huibian* (*Compilation of Biographies of Nationalities in Past Dynasties*). Beijing: Zhonghua Publishing House, 1957, p. 125. Wu was a state of The Three Kingdoms between 222 to 280 C.E.

21. Sima Qian. "Biographies of Farghana (Dawan Zhuan)," in *Shi Ji* (*Historical Memoirs*), Volume 10, 2nd ed. Beijing: Zhonghua Publishing House, 1982, p. 3162.

22. *Encyclopedia of Kazakhstan*, Volume 11, p. 401. Shokhan Välikhanov (1835–1865) is a famous Kazakh scholar, orientalist, historian, ethnologist, geographer, folklorist, teacher and democrat. During his early years he studied at the Kazakh school at Gusmurin and learned Arabic and Chaghatai. Subsequently he acquired a good knowledge of other Central Asiatic Turkic languages. In 1853 he completed his formal studies at the Omsk Cadet Academy. He lived in St. Petersburg for several years and led scientific expeditions to Central Asia and Xinjiang—to Kashgar, Aqsuw, Qulja, and other places.

23. Sima Qian. "Biographies of Farghana (Dawan Zhuan)," in *Shi Ji* (*Historical Memoirs*), 2nd edition. Beijing: Zhonghua Publishing House, 1982. Volume 123, p. 3168.

24. Ban Gu, *Han Shu* (*History of the Han Dynasty*) 96:2 p. 3901. Beijing: Zhonghua Publishing House, 1962.

25. Feng Cheng Jün. *Xiyu Diming* (*Geographical Names of Xiyu*). Expanded by Lu Junling. Beijing: Zhonghua Publishing House, 1980, p. 87.

26. Compilers Group. *Hasakezu Jian Shi* (*A Brief History of the Kazakh Nationality*). Urumqi: People's Publishing House of Xinjiang, 1987, p. 68.

27. Chen Yongling, ed. *Minzu Cidian* (*Dictionary of Nationalities*). Shanghai: Dictionary Publishing House, 1987, pp. 1018-1019.

28. Compilers Group. *Hasakezu Jian Shi* (*A Brief History of the Khazakh Nationality*). Urumqi: People's Publishing House of Xinjiang, 1987, p. 71.

29. *Ibid.*

30. *Ibid.*

31. *Kazakh Soviet Entsiklopedijasy* (*Kazakh Soviet Encyclopedia*), Volume 1, p. 451. Alma Ata: Kitap Publishing House, 1980.

32. *Jiu Tan Shu* (*History of the Tang Dynasty*) was written by Liu Xu during the time of Hou Jin (936–946). *Xin Tang Shu* is another historical compilation concerning the Tang, done by Ou-yang Xiu during Song times (960–1126).

33. See *Xin Tang Shu* (*Biographies of Xi Yu*), Bk. 2, for Khwari, Constantinopolitans, Bactriane, and Parsa. Sham refers to what is present-day Syria, and Khwari corresponds to what is now Khiva, south of the Aral Sea.

34. Anonymous. *Hudud al-Ghalam* (*The Regions of the World*), 372 A.H., translated and explained by V. Minorsky. Oxford: Oxford Univ. Press/Luzac and Co., 1937. Chinese transl. by Wang Zhilai and Zhou Xijuan. Xinjiang Social Science Academy, Central Asia Institute, pp. 121-122. Urumqi, 1983.

35. S. Amanzholov. *Voprocy Dialectologii i Istorii Kazakskogo Jazyka* (*Problems in Kazakh Linguistic History and Dialects*). Alma-Ata: Education Publishing House of KazSSR, 1959, 34–35.

36. In 582 C.E. the Turkish kaghanate was divided into a western and an eastern portion. The western portion, itself, was divided into two parts—a left (north) and a right (south). The Duwlat union of clans was situated in the left portion.

37. For a reference in a historical compilation from Song times (960-1126) see Ou-yang Xiu, *Xin Tang Shu: Dilizhi* (*Geographical Notes*). Beijing: Zhonghua Publishing House, 1975, part 7, 1130.

38. Compilers Group. *Hazakezu Jianshi/Khazakh Ultynyng Taryjhy* (*A Brief History of the Kazakh Nationality*). Beijing: Nationalities Printing House, 1987. Chinese edition, 81; Kazakh edition, 172.

39. Compilers Group. *Hasakezu Jian Shi* (*A Brief History of the Kazakh Nationality*). Urumqi: People's Publishing House of Xinjiang, 1987. p. 83.

40. Anonymous. *Hudud al-Ghalam* (*The Regions of the World*), Chinese transl. by Wang Zhi-Lai and Zhou Xijuan. Urumqi: Xinjiang Central Asia Institute of Social Science, 1983, 66.

41. *Weiwuerzu Lishi* (*History of the Uighur Nationality*), Chin. ed. by Liu Zhixiao. Bejing: Nationalities Publishing House, 1985, 139.

42. Rashid-al-din, *Jami al Tawarikh/She Ji* (*Collection of Histories*), Chin. ed., 1.1, p. 209. Beijing: Shang Wu Press, 1983. (Transl. from the Russian edition by Yu Dajun and Zhou Jianqi).

43. A handwritten collection of pedigree information collected in Xinjiang by the Social History Collection Group of the Xinjiang Minority Nationalities. (Estimated time span 1952-1957).

44. Rashid-al-din, *Jami al-Twarikh*, Chin. ed., 1.1, pp. 207-209.

45. See Wilhelm Barthold. *Zwölf Vorlesungen über die Geschichte der Türken Mittelasiens.* Hildesheim: Georg Olms Verlagsbuchhandlung, 1962. Chinese Translation by Luo Zhiping. Beijing: Social Science Publishing House of China, 1984.

46. Rashid-al-din, *Jami al Tawarikh*, Chin. ed., 1.1, p. 224.

47. Tajan khan and Bujrukh khan are both sons of Inanch Bilge Bughu khan. The two sons became hostile. Some Naimans followed Tajan and others followed Bujrukh. The latter was defeated by Chingis khan in 1202 C.E., and Tajan two years later. Tajan's wife and granddaughter were captured by Chingis khan; he married the granddaughter. See Rashid-al-din, *Jami al-Tawarikh*. Chin. ed., 1.1, p. 227.

48. See Rashid-al-din, *Jami al-Tawarikh*, Chin. ed., 1.2, pp. 251-252. See also Zhang Xinglang: *Zhong Xi Jiaotong Shiliao Huibian* (*Materials from the Historical Records of Traffic between China and Western Countries*) 5, p. 8. Beijing: Zhonghua Publishing House, 1977.

49. For the first three traditions see Compilers Group. *Khazakhtyng Khyskhasha Taryihy* (*A Brief History of the Kazakh Nationality*), Kazakh edition. Urumqi: People's Publishing House of Xinjiang, 1987, pp. 253-254. For the fourth tradition see S. Baisheva, editor. *Shezhire—Khazakhtyng Ruw-Taipalykh Khurylysy* (*Pedigree Structure of Kazakh Clans and Tribes*). Alma-Ata: Rawan Publishing House, 1991, pages 26-27.

50. Chen Yongling, ed. *Minzu Cidian* (*Dictionary of Nationalities*). Shanghai, 1987, p. 1244.

51. See "Alpamis," in *Khazakh Hyisalary* (*Kazakh Epics*), Volume 2, 520-700. Beijing: Nationalities Publishing House, 1984.

52. See Ä. Derbisälin, ed. "Muhabbat Nama," in *Kazakhstan.* Alma Ata: Science Publishing House, 1986, pp. 86-158.

53. Rashid-al-din, *Jami al-Tawarikh*, Chin. ed., 1.1, pp. 149-159.

54. Khadyrbek Zhünisbajev. *Orta Azia Men Khazakhstannyng Uly Ghalymdar* (*Famous Scholars of Central Asia and Kazakhstan*), Kazakh edition, Alma-Ata, 1964, pp. 270-279.

55. See *Codex Cumanicus*, archived in the library of St. Mark Church in Venice, Italy. Reference in Zengxiang Li, *An Introduction to Turkic Languages*. Beijing: Central Institute for Nationalities Press, 1992, p. 97.

Chapter 2

Spoken Blessings

The folk literature of the Kazakh people is rich in content, sagacious in thought, and vigorous in artistic expression. There are many types of stories, fantastic tales, as well as folksongs filled with passion and love. There are historical epics reciting the heroic adventures of Kazakh patriarchs and founders. There are poems that display the deeper roots of social coexistence, and proverbs that bristle with practical wit. There are myths and legends, tales about animals and fairies, and musings about a variety of customs. These include stories about Father Khorkhyt and anecdotes on glib tongued fellows like Zhirenshe, Aldar Köse, Khozha Nasyr, and Asan Khaighy. There are songs of pastoral nomadism, songs describing geography, songs about ancient customs, birth and marriage songs, and songs of mourning. Ecstatic librettos of solitary shamans—remnant echoes from antiquity—still resound at some distance from Islamic prayer chants and Islamicized Chinese traditions. In view of this great variety of fascinating ethnological materials, we have chosen to begin our collection with soberly spoken blessings *(bata)*.

Blessings or *bata* belong to the religious dimension. The word *bata* carries two meanings. Firstly, it means a prayer, either recited for a dead person or on other special occasions. Secondly, it refers to a general or formal blessing spoken as a greeting. Blessings or prayers

47

on behalf of the dead, and prayers for other occasions, will be presented in subsequent chapters of this book. General spoken blessings express well the religious ethos and confidence by which the Kazakh people, as a whole, approach their daily tasks and solve their problems—as they live under, and as they more or less consciously submit to, the governance of Allah.

Bata have evolved into a special genre of Kazakh folk literature, alongside proverbs and songs, and they must be taken seriously by folklorists. Blessings are spoken aloud, with poetic emotion and emphases. The speaker's most sincere feelings and wishes are thereby succinctly expressed. Such precision is possible because blessings are structured rather freely. Their syllables and rhymes are not arranged as rigidly as happens to be the case in most Kazakh songs and poems.

Long ago, when Kazakh warriors were sent on an expedition, and also when men went hunting, they were in the habit of asking directions from their elders and tribal heads. Words spoken by these tribal leaders are the oldest form of Kazakh blessings known. Nowadays the custom of reciting *bata* extends to all aspects of life. It has been combined with expressing hopes for social well-being and success in economic enterprises, for progress and improvement in the quality of life.

The Kazakhs speak blessings at all kinds of occasions, expecting good outcomes as a matter of course—before hunting, before slaughtering a sheep, a cow, or any other kind of animal, before and after dinner, before their children go to school, or before they become apprentices to learn a handicraft. They speak blessings before they undertake any significant or fresh venture.

Most often the blessings are recited by men, by adult men and by guests. When uttering a blessing the speaker raises his hands. He recites the appropriate words and concludes brushing with his palms downward over his face—using the Islamic prayer gesture. The other people who are present imitate this gesture. On grand occasions, frequently, a young man steps forth, raises his hands with palms facing upward. He asks the oldest man present to give the blessing, or to recite a *bata*. He concludes by loudly saying *ämjin* (Amen). After the blessing has been given, the people together respond with *Allahakpar!* (God is greatest!). With that culminating exclamation—the most powerful phrase recited by followers of Islam—the ritualized blessing concludes.

The contents of blessings vary in accordance with occasions and situations. The one given here has been recited on behalf of a newborn child. The fact that these particular words were spoken some time after Kalmyks (*Khalmakh*) of Jungaria (*Zhungar*) invaded Kazakh grasslands, can easily be inferred:

> Newborn baby—
> For your people grow!
> There is a tribe named Kerei,
> Be a *sheshen* among them,
> In your tribe there will be many disputes.[1]
> To your people be a leader.
> Your enemies are at the Zhungar side.[2]
> Be a hero who charges them singlehandedly.
> When you engage your enemies,
> Chop off their heads!
> *Allahakpar!*[3]

Our next blessing is spoken when a five-year-old Kazakh boy is recognized for mastering the skill of climbing onto a horse by himself. This Kazakh rite of passage will be explained in more detail in Chapter Four.

> While I am figuring your age,
> This year you are five.
> Upon your five-year horse
> Are embroidered all kinds of patterns.
> Owl feathers decorate this your five-year horse.
> We hope it will be under you forever.
> Be a worthy son of your people,
> May your name and honor never be tarnished.
> My dear Child! May your life be long,
> And your ideals be like mountains.
> Fire can be set on snowy ground,
> As long as there is someone to set it.
> As you find happiness yourself,
> Let bad luck depart from you.
> Stand before your age mates.
> Be happy, and rich in livestock.

But toward happiness be not a drunkard.
Be not a man with bloody hands.
Today I am ninety-five years old,
I am a man advanced in age.

Let me give you my bata:

May your age get to be as high as mine,
Let the spirits of your ancestors support you.
Let *Khyzyr* (Kezer) be your company.[4]
May Allah be your pillar.
Let Allah come and determine all matters for you.
Allahakpar![5]

Here follows a blessing that was recited by parents during an engagement which they had arranged:

My Relatives! You see we have an engagement,
May Allah sustain us.
Among the most happy occasions in the world,
Is there anything happier than becoming related by marriage?
Let us ask for the help of Allah.
Among relatives exist three tokens,
Although these are not everywhere the same:
White blessings, betrothal gifts, and sacred *neke,*
Three tokens since ancient times.[6]
May your hearts be beating together,
Be always arm in arm.
Let us all say Amen together.
We petition the one and only Allah.
Allahakpar![7]

A blessing recited for a newly married couple may establish the idea of nuptial happiness with words like these:

Your faces are smiling like the face of a child,
Your sleeping is as sweet as that of a young mother.
Be gentle and soft like a young girl,
As clear as the water of a fountain spring.
Be as grand and magnificent as mountains,
And your sounds as a morning lark singing.

Be profound and weighty as the deep sea,
While being alert and agile as an eagle.
Be a pair of sweethearts forever,
Inseparable as body and shadow.
Allahakpar![8]

Blessings may be spoken on behalf of a person who is assuming
an official position:

You just sit on your throne,
As we together cheer your happiness.
God placed thirty thousand families under your care,
The present is predestined by past struggles.
No one trusts his arms,
And the weights you carry are heavy.
In order to obtain esteem from your people,
To the high ones bow your head,
And to the poor ones show your mercy.
If two in disagreement come to you,
Do not simply take the side of the rich.
Distinguish what is high and low,
Distinguish what is lucky and unfortunate.
Take care of the hungry and the lean.
Allahakpar![9]

A blessing recited for a warrior who is on his way to battle may
go as follows:

May your campaign be pleasant!
May your words be very effective!
May your shots hit the target!
May your spear pierce the enemy!
May your battle steed run swiftly!
May your campaign bring loads of war trophies!
May your enemy be utterly hunted down!
May your troops remain always vigorous!
May your flag be fluttering in the breeze!
Allah will sustain you!
Allahakpar![10]

Blessings are recited not only for specific occasions, but also to satisfy general concerns of well-being and security:

> May no enemy be against your clan!
> May no disagreements arise between you and your people!
> May your pastures have plenty water and lush grass!
> May your settlement be a lucky place!
> May your hands be generous!
> May wherever you go be celebrations!
> May all your pack animals be camels!
> May all your milking stock be mares!
> May silk and satin be your clothing!
> May friends visit you in a continuous stream!
> May your enemies tremble before you!
> Allahakpar![11]

There are Kazakh blessings recited on behalf of individuals as well as for the whole of humankind. However, there also are certain left-handed blessings that may be spoken to satirize—in the name of Allah, just the same.

Blessings may be modified to ridicule a certain person for his bad behavior. Traditionally the Kazakh people maintained a simple nomadic economy. There were no trading establishments on their pasture lands. Survival depended on everyone's adherence to the nomadic rules of barter and hospitality. Every family was expected to welcome their guests warmly, and to feed them generously.

A man who came from another settlement could expect that his host family would serve him dinner and would let him stay in their home overnight. To welcome a stranger, one should slaughter a sheep or at least serve him stewed mutton. Doing otherwise meant to put the guest down, to humiliate him together with the entire settlement that he represented. Accordingly, there have been composed *bata*, designed especially for niggardly hosts. A tale is told about a guest—always an unidentified guest—who visited the home of an unnamed typically stingy rich man, one who owns much livestock. For his guest he slaughtered and cooked a sick sheep, an animal whose body was infested with worms. Before slaughtering the guest recited this blessing:

This three- or four-year-old sheep—
Does it carry a gun on its neck? Is it a hunter?[12]
If by chance there is a battle, it might be useful.
O my Excellency! By my word! Do not slaughter it!
Allahakpar![13]

"Once upon a time" another stranger came to the home of a typical greedy rich man who owned much livestock. The wealthy host, instead of slaughtering a sheep ordered his wife to cook gruel for their guest. After dinner a son of the host stood up, with outstretched hands, and said "Amen"—in proper manner he asked the guest to recite the blessing. The guest's rejoinder went like this:

You spread your arms and said "Amen."
For your one-year-old colt you said a *bata*.[14]
I have not eaten the meat. I ate gruel.
So, I can only recite an ordinary *bata*.
You asked me to say "Amen," my Child!
What did you give to me—
Standing there and stretching forth your hands?
What can I say to you?
Who has ever seen such a thing?
Gruel you gave to me.
You asked me to give my blessing, I will do so:

May the dogs eat your sausages!
Look at the meat in your cupboard.
And look at the faces who sit here without shame.
Allahakpar![15]

Regrettably, tales that feature such plots—rowdily inverted blessings bordering on curses—generally end as cliff-hangers. They never tell us what happened next. Surely, listeners who have enjoyed the simple plot of such a tale always are left to wonder—should an occasion arise—whether they themselves would dare to recite such an inverted blessing. They knew, of course, that in following through they would convert a blessing into a curse. Didactic tales of this sort aim at teaching nomadic hospitality—not necessarily Kazakh etiquette for self-righteous guests.

Notes

1. A *sheshen* is a man with fluent speech, able to negotiate disputes.
2. "Zhungar" refers to the Kalmyk people of Jungaria.
3. Selected by Awelkhan Hali from among materials kept in the Xinjiang branch of the Society for Folk Literature and Art of China.
4. In Kazakh legends, *Khyzyr* (Kezer) is a benevolent celestial being with a white beard. He brings good fortune.
5. Xinjiang branch of the Society for Folk Literature and Art of China.
6. Betrothal gifts are given by the groom's family to the bride's family. *Neke* means "marriage," and *neke* verses from the Qur'an are recited to establish the proper relationship between husband and wife.
7. Xinjiang branch of the Society for Folk Literature and Art of China.
8. *Ibid.*
9. *Ibid.*
10. *Ibid.*
11. *Ibid.*
12. To prevent a sick sheep from licking its wounds, Kazakh herders put a wooden yoke on the sheep's neck. Here the guest satirizes the yoke on that sick sheep as a disease-shooting "gun"—implying that the host was aiming this gun at him. He therefore emphasizes the greater usefulness of such an animal to the host himself, in doing battle against an acknowledged enemy, some day.
13. From the Altai region, collected by Awelkhan Hali.
14. Kazakh people serve colt meat only to their most privileged guests. The blessing supposedly was spoken on behalf of the colt that was never slaughtered.
15. From the Altai region, collected by Awelkhan Hali.

Chapter 3

A World to Sing About

A Kazakh proverb contemplates, "When you are born, songs open the door to your life; when you fall into eternal sleep, songs accompany you to the grave." Between these two delimiting moments in a human life, practically at all conceivable life situations, Kazakh folk songs add decorum. They accompany every rite of passage and help define many of life's fleeting moments.

The general demeanor of Kazakh people is cheerful, energetic, and direct. Their lyrics express this temper and embrace with it all aspects of life. When someone gets married, joyous wedding songs are intoned; at funerals sorrowful dirges of lament can be heard. When a baby is born one sings birthing songs; and when herders move to other pastures, moving songs are vocalized. There are professional bards *(akhyndar)* who sing songs and accompany these on the *dombra*.[1] Still today some of them can be found, reciting ancient epic poetry.

Odes *(Zhyr)*

Odes are hearty expressions of innate confidence and devotion. They are forceful songs, intoned by the Kazakh people in praise of their native land, their relatives, their livestock, and toward their own well-being. For example, in a song titled "Golden Mountain" *(Altyn Taw)* the people of Akhsay county, in Gansu, sing:

Heartily I sing, standing on the southern slope of Akhsay.
I want to write my words on white paper:
Pine trees are green forever,
And beautiful as gardens.[2]

A song in praise of a certain "Clear Mountain Spring" expresses emotional attachments and love toward this spring:

We cannot find another spring the water of which
Is as sweet and clear as yours!

Kazakh odes are uplifting to the degree that a description of their purpose is best left to the wings of poetry and song. Prose commentary will never come close. After all...

People in this world should sing without ceasing.
They should be happy and joyous,
They should not be devoured by the world of darkness.

Songs of Grievance

There are, nevertheless, songs which express mourning and nostalgia for better days. While Kazakh people think fondly about their native places, and while they cherish the memory of their dead relatives, they frequently also erupt with singing songs of lament about their own misfortunes. Emotional boldness breaks forth as they relive suffering, as simultaneously they insist afresh on a happier life. So for example, concerning the 1930s, Kazakh voices sing:

There was no impartiality in those dark years.
Our people suffered and fled far away.
Some fled abroad and passed their lives in misery.
They hope to return to their homelands.

Kazakh songs of lament express how the people were forced to
wander about, aimlessly and forlorn at times, in strange and unfamiliar
lands. And doing so they cherished, in song at least, the memory of
their native places and their relatives. In "Xinjiang My Native Land"
they sing:

Xinjiang, my native land!
You are the place of my birth and initiation.
Friends of my childhood, grown up together,
Severed now, each lives somewhere far, far away.
I climb to the mountain top and look at you,
Everywhere are Gobi landscapes of desolation.
I long for our relatives in Xinjiang,
I loose control over my feelings,
My breast is wet with tears.[3]

Love Songs

Songs are a proper means by which young Kazakh lovers express
their fascination for each other. These songs extol the handsomeness of
the lad and the beauty of the girl. They tend to liken love to the
radiance of gold or to the breadth and depth of waters in the lake. They
address the beloved as "My Sun" and, if separated, they lament
because their "heart will break."

Young people pour into love songs their innermost feelings.
Separation from a loved one is a frequent occurrence in Kazakh life.
In search of pasture for their herds they must move often. Means of
travel are scarce. Accordingly, in their songs of love they express the
agony of separation. They sing about their mutual hopes for a safe
return and reinforce their song with a blessing. Here is the love song
titled "Sweetheart" *(Zhan Erke)*.

Your homestead has moved away,
How despondent I feel.

Leaving you behind,
It causes me to lose my composure.
How are you, my dear Aikhara!
I miss you very much, Oh my Sweetheart.
A long time I have not seen you.
I now graze my sheep and cattle
On the opposite slope of the mountain.[4]

Work Songs *(Engbek Zhyry)*

There also are songs to sing while caring for one's livestock. The Kazakhs are herders, and this is the reason why most of their work songs are about the raising of livestock. These songs express the immediacy of life in the real world—while delivering lambs, while milking cows or mares, while shearing wool or while rolling felt.

A song intoned while driving animals to their summer pasture may go like this:

Heartily I sing the song of grazing lands.
Livestock I graze, and I lust for our summer pasture.

A simple song that is chanted during lambing season may feature words like these:

We are busy delivering lambs,
And occupied with all kinds of work.
The butter we make from the milk is sweet,
And tasty like honey.

During that busy season, milking women may sing "lamb suckling" *(töyge)* songs to mother sheep, encouraging them to let the milk flow for their lambs:

Töyge, töyge, my Sheep.
Töyge, töyge, my Sheep, töyge.
Töyge, töyge, töyge, töyge.
Take, my Sheep! Take your child!
Oh this is your own-born child!

Töyge, töyge, my Sheep.
Töyge, töyge, töyge.[5]

Aside from such songs for sheep, there are similar ones chanted to mother camels or to mother cows. The basic tunes and words of endearment to each animal species are the same. Only the names of the mother animals and their young are adjusted to refer to the kind of animal that presently is being milked.

Kazakh herders understand their animals in environmental contexts, as being quite analogous to humankind. Animals have their own gods, and Kazakh herders respect those deities, as well as the relationship that exists between the animals and their divine masters. Such religious respect not only assures the well-being of domestic animals, but facilitates the justification for human ownership as well. They regard such deities as *ije,* that is, as Lords or primary Owners of the animals. They also refer to these divine animal masters as *piri* or Immortal Ones. Collectively they may be addressed with *Tängri,* that is, Heaven or God.

Mentioned individually, the lord of sheep is Shopan Ata (Father or Grandfather Shopan). The lord of goats is Seksek Ata (Father Seksek). The lord of cows is Zenggi Baba (Father Zenggi). The lord of horses is Zhylkhyshy Ata (Father Zhylkhyshy) or Khambar Ata (Father Khambar). The divine lord of camels is Oisyl Khara (Great Oisyl).[6] All these divine masters are credited with securing peace, and with bestowing fertility upon livestock. They are believed to create prosperity and happiness for the people.

Owing to their intimate relationship with herd animals, as human counterparts to divine animal masters, Kazakh people have, since ancient times, regarded their domestic animals as a kind of people. Animals are believed to have their own awareness of life, and even have their own language.

It is still not uncommon today for people to express their personal sentiments of happiness and joy, or their sorrow and grief, to their animals by way of human words. Also, in a roundabout way, the elders tell stories that express love toward their children with words channeled through the mouths of animals. In this manner, so as not to show excessive love toward their little ones, they avoid the risk of losing authority. All the same, the children are sensitized to a point where they develop empathy not only toward story animals, but also toward live pet animals, as well as respect for their elders who communicate this wisdom as being something worthwhile.

Every second line in the following poem completes an analogy and thereby teaches the universality of the parent-child relationship. Parental love is a natural ingredient in the entire animal kingdom.

> Sheep loves its child and calls it my Brown One (Khongyr);
> Nothing you understand, O my Dear One (Momyn).
> Goat loves its child and calls it my Kid (Lakh);
> Jumping from here to there, O my Small-eared One (Shunakh).[7]
> Cow loves her child and calls it my Torpakh;
> When night falls you do not stir, O my Timid One (Khorkhakh).[8]
> Horse loves its child and calls it my Foal (Khulyn);
> You run like a winged steed, O my Weakling (Zhuryn).
> Camel loves its child and calls it my Botash.
> Your eyes are beaming, O my Wild One (Totash).[9]

These songs about animals and children move beyond the mere recognition of analogous attributes. They even place human children under the protection of pre-Islamic divine animal guardians.[10] In this manner they teach good behavior at home and discourage children from running away from home too far.

> The child of sheep is my Khongyr,
> Do not break your nest, my Well-behaved.
> (Grand)father Shopan bless and protect you,
> O my Lamb (Khoshakhan), where are you?
> *Pushait! Pushait!*[11]

> You pull out a hair from it, and it will bleat,
> Calling its (Grand)father Seksek.
> Growing up on the grasslands,
> Bouncy and Lively One, where are you?
> *Shöre! Shöre!*[12]

> She gives us milk like a flowing fountain,
> On moving day she lends us her strength.
> Zenggi Baba bless and protect you,

My Good One, where are you?
Awhaw! Awhaw![13]

Antiphonal Songs *(Aitys)*

Another type of Kazakh folk song features antiphonal poetic dialogue. Such songs are numerous today, and they are constantly being renewed and added to. Rhymed, musical antiphonal dialogue is a tradition that is still very much alive. It may be regarded as the cradle of Kazakh folk literature. Many a Kazakh poet's mind has first been stimulated when engaged in youthful song and poetry contests while composing *aitys*.

Comparing humankind with animals not only helps parents understand and cope with children—as though they were some especially dear kind of pets—but also helps young people explain the ultimate origins of all living creatures. By way of origin stories the riddles of life and creation are gradually learned and naturalized. When maturing boys and girls meet, they meet to sing—of course:

Boy: It is wonderful for a young fellow to ride on a horse.
Distinguished he looks while galloping around a girl's *awyl*.
If you are an *akhyn* (bard) with a glib tongue,
Please answer me. How was the cow created?

Girl: At age ten I began attending song contests,
At place of an akhyn there is much joy.
If your knowledge is meager, then let me tell you,
The cow was created from water, at the very beginning.

Boy: I may be standing or lying down—you, Dear, are on my mind.
Do you believe that I am telling you the truth?
It is one of the animal wonders,
Please answer me, where does the sheep come from?

Girl: I grew up in a family, and I am a pet.
Like you, I attended song contests early in life.
A wonderful smell floated to the people's nose.
When the sheep was created in Mecca, at the very beginning.

Boy: Do you agree with what I am singing, my Dear One?
      Please give me a piece of your scarf,
      Wings of heroes and pride of men, since ancient times.
      Please answer me, what is the horse made of?

Girl: If you find the path, it makes the arduous journey,
       Under its belt clouds of dust are raised.
       If your knowledge is meager, then let me tell you,
       The horse is made of wind running swiftly.

Boy: While the spring water flows, sparkling,
      O my Dear One, my heart feels disconsolate.
      If you are an akhyn, a good singer,
      Find me the answer. Of what is the camel made?

Girl: From left to right my songs never cease,
       Don't fall from the road while saying "my Dear."
       If your knowledge is meager, then let me tell you,
       The camel was made of saline soil, at the very beginning.[14]

Cosmogonic notions alluded to in this song are endorsed by themes found in a variety of Kazakh folk tales. Cow, sheep, horse, and camel are the four primary domestic animals, and these were created at the beginning in Mecca—of water, wind, and salt. While such sagacious statements may not seem completely factual, then let it at least be known that water, wind, and salt are nicknames of these animals. After all, the cow likes to drink water; it will drink wherever water can be found. Sheep were introduced from Arabia. The horse gallops as fast as the wind. And the camel likes to lick salt and to eat grasses grown on saline soil.

Mixed groups representing different settlements, or groups of boys versus groups of girls, square off during large public gatherings. The audience chooses the winner. Success and failure are generally decided on the basis of which side gets tongue-tied first. Here is an example of an *aitys* song contest between groups of girls and boys:

Girls: My *awyl* moves to new pasture—at Khara Suw (Black River).
        How happy our herders are!

Alyi-dai, Alyi-dai, Oh! Sing!
Young men, Alyi-dai, dai!

Boys: We only sing with young people,
Our songs rush swiftly like mountain streams.
Having a chance to be here with you, young girls,
How thoroughly delighted we are.

Girls: Your voices are,
Just like old men sighing.
If you do not know how to sing,
Let our horses teach you neighing.

Boys: Your singing is but gibberish,
Neither melody nor lofty words are in your song.
If you do not know how to sing,
Let us embrace you and teach you.[15]

Forefathers of the Kazakhs chose poetry as the medium through which they would pass on to posterity their knowledge of society, and samples of common sense, as well as skills of survival. It may be argued that all Kazakh poems and songs do communicate or teach something.

The bards of old have tried to explain not only the origins of various clans or tribes, but along with these comes the history of the entire Kazakh confederation. Of course, such "histories" are limited in scope by what poetic structures are able to carry. Nevertheless, the general pattern of Kazakh prehistory, of history and of the people's quest for identity, their memory of significant heroes, and the formation of the Kazakh nationality with their emergence from a sea of tribes and nations, are reflected adequately enough.

The Kazakh people have a saying: "One who does not know seven generations of his forefathers, shows that he is an orphan." This means that every Kazakh person who has grown up in an ordered family should know the "family tree" of his or her *ruw* (clan or tribe) and should also know how the history of this tribe fits into the history of the larger *zhüz* (horde). Kazakh children, one generation after another, enter the tribal consciousness and community by way of poetic recitations of their genealogies.

During antiphonal singing each side refers to its own clan or tribe with great pride, in an unconcealed effort to surpass the other. We present here a sample of such a contest.

Singers from the Arghyn and Naiman tribes confront each other in friendly contest. This tradition of competitive artistry certainly has led to many more constructive results than going to war could have produced. About the traditional alternative, warfare, Kazakh epics have much to tell. For wholesome contrast we therefore travel here along the path of song, of harmony and peace. The singers representing the Arghyn tribe begin:

> In case you do not know, let me tell you,
> Arghyn has a boundless stretch of grassland.
> From this side to yonder is a month journey,
> Seven large portions are there.
> The rich men are Baieke, Dosan, Khanai,
> Aitkhusan, Nurmuhamet, Tursyn and Zhanai.
> Their herds of livestock, in huge mountain ranges,
> Are seen grazing as far as your eyes can see.
> If I led you and showed you, would you be interested?
> Musa and Shorman are our financiers,
> Their institutions, wealthy, have never been depleted.
> Musa's own son was Sadwakas,
> He saved many eagles (good men) who had fallen into nets.
> There is not anyone like Khazankhap,
> All of his ancestors were great men.[16]
> Not long after he was born
> He became chief of a thousand families.
> Not a single Kazakh can compare with Allahbergen,
> If compared they cannot surpass him.
> Tölebai took on his duties after him.
> Good deeds done for Naiman are never to be forgotten.
> In your Naiman tribe no one is like Tättimbet,
> His fingers could pluck forty songs,
> He was born to be a singer and a man of wealth.[17]
> If I were to sing about them all, you would not last.
> Is there anyone like Alsynbai in your clan?
> Ten Naimans cannot compare with him.
> He made a name for himself as a *khazy*.[18]

He sat on the khan's throne and was never moved.
Khazhy Khunanbai was a White-shoulder among the people,
He was able to look down upon all.[19]
The wise men of Naiman gazed at him,
They were unable to trim a single hair from his head.
Ibrahim's name was well known among Kazakhs,
Created by God he was a cut above others,
He became famous throughout the whole tribe,
He was a just man who could split a hair into two.[20]
All clansmen of Naiman cannot compare with Abai,
The greatness of his wisdom spread far and wide,
He opened the mouth of the fountain of knowledge,
From his youth unswervingly his mind clung firmly to truth.[21]

From the song of the Arghyn singers one could learn the names of famous men in their tribe. Most of these were clan chiefs. They are remembered, and are presented in song contests, for having contributed to Kazakh survival and culture. From narrations about famous men in the past, as these singers have presented, one glimpses at least some rough outline of Kazakh general fortunes throughout history. While in most lands "history is competition among storytellers," here it is competition among singers and poets as well.

Of course, in order to obtain a fairer perspective it is absolutely necessary to listen to the songs of other tribes as well. Here is the reply of the Naiman singers:

From Naiman to Kharakerei: Syban, Muryn,
Shörebai, Tana, Hero Täwkebai,
And Zholymbet—God's glory be with them![22]
What Kazakh dared to speak in their presence?
From Täkün was Khozybai, and Tilewberdi
Whose son is Ädilkhan, known to everyone.
God gave him quick advancement in his career,
From among the people, he became their khan.
Are my Naiman forefathers less than those of Arghyn?
All kinds of crafts they taught their people.[23]
Who can compare with our Barakh?
He was the master of Khuttybai and Baizhigit.
Who can compare with Khabanbai of great ability?
From generation to generation his skills were passed,

From Khadyrbai to Alyizhakhsy and Ädilbek,
And onward to his son Süleimen.[24]

The competitive nature of this antiphonal singing is readily apparent. Not only is the reputation of one tribe displayed for comparison with that of another, and not only are the heroes of one tribe invoked to match or surpass their counterparts elsewhere—in the final analysis it is the singers who wrap themselves into the ancient glories of their respective tribes. After all, their own tribes are their primary audiences, and from these audiences comes the applause that supports the singers' fame.

About Geography

In ancient times the so-called "mountain songs" or "geographical songs" of the Kazakh oral tradition corresponded to what, in later written traditions, would become geography textbooks and atlases. By way of these songs traditional Kazakh people taught each other about geographical sites, resources, and variations in climate over their vast realms:

The native land of our tribe (Kerei) is Altai Sawyr,
It contains good places, better than any other land.
All people there love their native places,
They love the soil upon which they were born and raised.
They were raised between Ertis and Nura rivers.
Springs of water bubble forth at many places,
Flowers bloom beautifully, and people are in ruddy health.
The wealth of the land is inexhaustible for thousands of epochs.
Altai Mountain is the father of those that surround him.
Ülinggir is a hide bag *(saba)* full of *khymyz* (kumiss).
Trees from which to carve nice wooden bowls and *pispeks*
Are grown along the sides of streams,
Which at their lower ends flow into huge Lake Ülinggir.[25]
Livestock and fishes are equally abundant.
The two side-ranges of Sawyr Mountain,
Salbyrty and Narynkhara, are surrounded by the lake.
The summit of Sawyr Mountain touches the sky,
And around its top floats a sea of clouds.

The place is cool in summer and warm in winter,
People who move there love the summer pasture.
The ridge of Altai Range is higher than others,
Stag and doe are playing in its bosom.
On the other side is the yellow grassland of Uranghai,
There elk and moose are roaming.[26]
The source of Kharaertis River is Khajyrty—
When you remember her, your tears will not stop.[27]
The area is good for planting and herding,
Is good for raising food and drink.
Sarsümbe is a city at the source of Khyran River,
Nearby is a grassland, Shemirshek.
Domestic trouble and foreign invasion together have struck,
They plunder your livestock once a year.
To the east, and far away, is a hot spring,
When you see it you know that it is a wonderful place.
Birds cannot fly nor men climb over mountains so high.
Next to that hot spring are high cliffs.
Kätingki, Emegeiti, and Kiting evergreens—
A primeval forest of various kinds of evergreen.
It looks like the skilled work of able hands,
Scenery such as this is magnificent.
Ermegeiti and Khalwyn are contiguous.
Mineral water from there can cure diseases.
Golden Altai is known throughout the whole world,
Her treasures and wealth are uncountable.
Bölekei, Sholakai, Üshkhurylystai,
And Maitöbe were enchanted by their grasslands.
At the center of Maitöbe a meeting was held,
Bukhash was district official, Bayeke lost the election.
Alkhabek and Bilezik are twin grasslands,
Herds of livestock there are fat and strong.
At the mountain top is a lake,
Natural resources of Khomkhanas are as rich as the ocean.
Kendirlik and Dolandy also are situated nearby,
The nose of Saikhan Mountain sticks forth between them.
The summer pastures of two clans are there,
Divided into two portions by Ice Mountain.[28]

The natural features and geographical character of the Altai region are masterfully painted by the words and colorful phrases of this poem. The description of Sawyr and Ülinggir is graphic and awesome. The political realism is striking—as the collection of livestock taxes, once a year, is likened to being invaded by foreigners—to being plundered by enemy peoples.

About Fishes

The subject matter of common interest between adults and children in Kazakh herder society are, understandably, their domestic animals—sheep, goats, cows, horses, and camels. Proverbial wisdom has it that "livestock is the pillar of Kazakh life." However, some wild animals along the periphery of the herders' domain do roam, fly, or swim into the arena of the Kazakh imagination as well.

Because all along, Kazakhs have been living in Inner Asia, and because there they have been nomadic herders foremostly, they know very little about the variety that exists among species of fishes *(balykh)*. Kazakh herders traditionally have regarded anyone who engaged in fishing or planting as paupers—with a considerable measure of disdain. Names of several fishes in the Kazakh language are therefore difficult to trace, and descriptions of them in folklore are vague. Kazakh knowledge about fish may on that account seem negligible to outsiders. But something that is not very well known, nevertheless, can be sung about for the sheer pleasure of rhythm, melody, and sketchy vocabulary. And whatever it is that is communicated about nineteen species of fish does reveal to outsiders at least a measure of encyclopedic curiosity—of rational human beings who also happen to enjoy singing.

In the hands of mullahs are copies of the Qur'an.
Where water dries up the fishes will die.
If you do not know it, please listen, I tell you.
Fishes who live in water are nineteen kinds.

Please listen to my song, and stick up your ears.
We have no real knowledge because we are poor.
So if you too are ignorant, let me tell you and remember:
The biggest fish is the *Nahan* fish.

The second largest is *Zhajyn* (Whale),
What he eats are those next to him.
The number of fishes who equal him, is small.
That is why its name is *Zhajyn*.

The third biggest fish is *Metire*,
And he lives in the rapids.
If you hang him under your roof,
His tail reaches the ground.

The fourth largest fish is called *Khurtkha,*
Everybody knows its name.
Cooked its meat is sweet, and its broth is hot.
While you taste it, be careful not to burn your lips.

The fifth is called the *Khyzyl* Fish (Red Snapper).
As huge as a camel, it is a long fish.
When you smoke its meat it tastes like horse meat.
People love it, no doubt.

The sixth big fish is called *Shortan* (Pike),
Shortan-fish is of medium size.
His back is spotted, belly white, and pointed is his mouth.
His temperament is more brusque than that of other fishes.

The seventh one is called *Akh,*
Akh-fish is washed white in rapids.
Those who know such secrets
Deem themselves terrific and are swollen with pride.

The eighth fish is *Khara*-fish (Black Dolphin),
It is a fish with great intelligence.
While, O how wonderful, it plays in the water,
Its temperament is always that of a child.

The ninth fish is *Sazan*-fish.
Whoever tastes it will be full of praise.

Let me catch some for you from the water.
Set up a fire and cook it with skill.

The tenth fish is *Iyt*-fish (Dog-fish),
Everyone knows it very well.
When the earth was drowned by the flood,
A maggot was left and transformed into *Iyt*-fish.

The eleventh fish is *Akh Khairan*.
Where *Akh Khairan* is, water turns muddy.
Because its meat is so sweat,
Many people love it.

The twelfth fish is *Sary*-fish (Yellow Croaker).
People enjoy the sight of it.
If you also want to enjoy it,
Come with me and I will show you.

The thirteenth fish is *Taban*-fish (Crucian Crab).
It moves slower than other fishes.
You know there are no fins under its stomach.
How can we say that this animal is bad?

The fourteenth fish is *Bughy* (Deer Fish).
It likes to hide at water's bottom.
It catches smaller ones than itself,
It swallows and gobbles them up in one go.

The fifteenth fish is *Taspa*-fish.
Lots of them are in the sea.
People who have seen it say it is not fish,
It is just like the belt of a horse's saddle.

The sixteenth fish is *Lakha*-fish,
Fins grow up from its head.
While frogs and fishes divided their realms,
Frogs chose the lake, and *Lakha* chose the sea.

The seventeenth fish is *Bürge* (Flea-fish),
The tongues of fishes and frogs are the same.
In this world, fishes number the most,
Whether lakes or rivers, they are full of them.

The eighteenth fish is *Shabakh* (Fry Fish),
Where there is water there is *Shabakh*.
Fishes are natural resources, the wealth of water.
They are food for humankind, inexhaustible.

The nineteenth fish is *Alakhanat* (Mullet, Barracuda).
It flies as the birds and has fins to swim.
I told you about the variety of fishes, one by one.
Please learn them from my song, and tell others.[29]

Fish songs are sometimes chanted in musical dialogue, responsively. An average Kazakh may or may not be able to sing a fish song. If he knows one, the number of fishes about which he can tell something will depend on his scope of general knowledge. Fish songs have been added to Kazakh song contests, primarily to exhibit and to measure talent and general knowledge.

Poems of Falsehood

From the credulity-taxing taxonomy of fishes—which was recited more for teasing the human imagination than for enlightenment—it is a small step to letting the imagination fly a trifle farther and soar a little freer. The result is nonesense songs for sheer entertainment.

Knowledge always comes in two forms—as propositions that claim truth and as stimuli by means of which opposites may be dragged into view. A reflection on opposites from the perspective of what generally is accepted will generate surprises. And surprises, in turn, inspire young and old *homines sapientes* during all kinds of joyous occasions. A typical "opener" for singing falsehood songs is the tale about a certain chieftain:

Once upon a time there lived a khan who was caught up in boredom and meaningless inactivity, day in and day out. So he requested that falsehood lyrics be sung for his amusement. Nobody knew how to do this. So the khan had a better idea and offered a challenge:

"Who can sing falsehood songs for me, with forty different falsities? I will marry my daughter to him, and let him be my prime minister to boot."

The requirement was not to include a single true statement. The khan would chop off the head of anyone who failed. In spite of the risk involved, many young men desired the khan's daughter and wanted to be the khan's prime minister. They tried, and because their songs included true statements their heads were chopped off. One day there came a poor shepherd boy. He sang a song with forty different falsities and won the prize. Here is a sample from his repertoire:

The skill of my tongue is not to tell you lies,
Think about it whether what I say are truths or lies.
They counted and took away forty mares as betrothal gift,
When I gave my daughter to a pheasant—a yurt in addition.

Using the skull of a canary we built the yurt,
From the long hairs of mosquitos I twisted the cords.
Forty crows and thirty bees came as matchmakers,
Dragonfly accepted the gifts from his relatives.[30]

A frog married his daughter to a butterfly,
And the bottle fly acted as matchmaker between them.
We caught a fat ant and slaughtered,
Held the wedding ceremony and horse races that went with it.

When yet unborn I was rich in the four kinds of livestock,
I sold all of them for my father to get married.
I knew how to raise livestock from early on,
That is why now I am so poor.

The first time I went to my relatives I rode on a crow.
Before their other sons-in-law arrived,
I caught a male locust to ride on,
To show my riding skills to my father-in-law....[31]

As the Kazakhs all along have been cherishing serious poetry and songs, so to this day they also have loved falsehood poems. The example, of which excerpts are being offered next, has only recently been featured at an antiphonal song contest. The lines that contain references to harvester machines and tractors make obvious the recent date of their composition. Full participation in the old Kazakh literary genre, of falsehood songs, is nevertheless successfully maintained.

I am here to speak from the depth of my heart,
If in a thousand statements you find fault, mine are flawless.
When I was thirsty I drank the Sairam lake,[32]
Oh, I emptied it and it did not quench my thirst...

I planted fried wheat into sand.
From each *mu* I reaped one thousand five hundred pounds.[33]
While reaping I hitched a rabbit to the combine,
For its nose-string I used the mustache of a rat.

In our hometown the milk of birds flows freely to form lakes.
To gather sheep wool we use a wheat combine.
Is not this the prosperity of our *awyl*?
Castrated sheep bore one lamb and uncut rams bore two...

The length of my wife's beard is two *khulash*,[34]
Without pains her oldest son was born, drunk.
His umbilical cord uncut, he stood and taught other children.
Even if my other words are falsehood, these are true...

Without suffering a tractor has died.
Because of grief we sang dirges and cried.
While we were reading *Zhanaza* prayers,
He woke up and recovered consciousness....[35]

Suddenly an idea flashed through my mind,
I wanted to go to the yonder side of sky.
Without hoe or spade, I used the molar of a fish,
I dug a hole through the sky and peeped.

Whales over there were very hungry,
When I fed them for one and two days.
Süleimen's ring was lost (over there),
I found it in the clouds and gave it back to him.

The earth is like a wooden basin.
I closed my eyes and it appeared clear.
The stars are ear rings of beautiful girls.
I picked up two and gave them to my daughter.[36]

Falsehood poems dwell on impossibilities. They provide a license to think what, in the seriousness of everyday life, would be unthinkable. After the manner of ceremonial clowns elsewhere in tribal cultures, the Kazakh bards who recited falsehood poems have widened the people's horizon—if not their horizon of the physical world, then at least the hypothetical horizons of imagination. A playful free mind is destined to find food, or gems, or happiness, sooner or later:

When three years old, I was engaged in hunting.
With straw bullets I shot and killed a thousand wild horses.
I used spider webs to weave a tapestry,
Sold it for hundred-ninety and was not begrudged.

I hoisted six pillars to sustain the sky.
Sponsoring a ceremony I slaughtered thousands of mosquitoes.
I divided one heart of them into four pieces, and ate.
That was the first time in my life I felt full.

The son of a stallion is a (wolf)-whelp.
Even if you kill me I will not tell you a lie.
A thousand people were riding on a single rat.
Hey! With a kick it killed all of them.

I made a silver shoe for a white rat
From the fur of a mole's tail which I use for my collar.
I skinned a yellow mosquito in its entirety,
To make a *saba*, to be filled with mare's milk *(khymyz)*.[37]

Notes

1. A dombra is a stringed instrument of the lute family. The Kazakh version features two strings.

2. This stanza, and the three that follow, were collected by Li Zengxiang in Akesai Kazakh Autonomous County, Gansu, summer 1959.

3. Such songs were sung by Kazakhs in Akesai during the rule of Sheng Shicai (1933-1943). Between 1936 and 1939 many Kazakh people moved from Xinjiang to Akesai. Collected in Akesai Kazakh Autonomous County, Gansu, in the summer of 1959.

4. This and the next two stanzas were obtained by Awelkhan Hali, from the files of the People's Publishing House of Xinjiang.

5. Collected in Akesai Kazakh Autonomous County, Gansu, summer 1959.

6. The words *ata, baba,* and *khara* all imply the qualities of great, grand, or ancient. They imply an amplitude of greater-than-mortal ancestors and divine grandfathers. The etymology of most names of these divinities is not known. Only *Shopan* may be traced to a Persian loanword related to *chopan, chuwpan, chuban, chuwban* or *shaban*. He is the divine grandfather of sheep. Nowadays *Shopan* has become the title of a poultry raiser.

7. In comparison with the kid of a goat, a human baby has comically small ears.

8. A *torpakh* is a calf from six to ten months old.

9. See Anonymous. *Istoria Kazakskoi Literatury 1*, p. 37. Alma Ata: Izdatel'stvo Akademii Nawk Kazakskoi, 1948. A *bota* is a small camel. The *-sh* suffix signifies endearment.

10. Divine animal guardians, masters, and owners are gods who survived from the evolutionary stratum of early hunters and gatherers. Some of these deities were rediscovered with modified functions during the era of domestication and herding.

11. *Pushait* is a call with which one lures the sheep. (Grand)father Shopan is the deity that protects sheep.

12. *Shöre* is the proper call to lure goats. (Grand)father Seksek is the divine protector of goats.

13. From the files of the People's Publishing House of Xinjiang. *Awhaw* is the exclamation for calling cows. Zenggi Baba is the protector deity of cows.

14. Anonymous. *Zhigitke Öner De Öner Öleng De Öner*. Urumqi: Peoples Publishing House of Xinjiang, 1989, 350-352.

15. Collected by Li Zengxiang in 1956, in Zhemenai County, Altai Prefecture, from Orazbai Ahmetbek-uly, a forty-nine year old herder.

16. Khazankhap, Allahbergen, and Tölebai were chiefs of the Arghyn tribe.

17. Naiman is the name of the tribe represented by the opposite group of singers. Tättimbet is a famous singer and dombra player.

18. A *khazy* is a Muslim appointed to preside over an Islamic court of law.

19. "Khazhy" (Haji) means pilgrim, and in a more specific sense it refers to a Muslim who has completed a pilgrimage to Mecca. Khunanbai, Abai's father, was chief of a clan. A White-shoulder *(Ukhykhty Adam)* is someone who has authority and power.

20. "Ibrahim" was the Islamic name of Abai who lived from 1845 to 1904. He became famous as a Kazakh poet and thinker and was chief of the Tobykhty clan.

21. Folk Literature and Art Society of China, Xinjiang Branch.

22. These are chiefs and forefathers of the Naiman tribe.

23. The Naiman people have the reputation of being highly skilled craftsmen.

24. Folk Literature and Art Society of China, Xinjiang Branch.

25. A *pispek* is a wooden stick used to pound mare's milk during the fermentation process which turns the milk into *khymyz* (sometimes transliterated as "kumiss").

26. "Uranghai" is the Kazakh name for Tuva or the Tuvinians.

27. That area has been captured by the Mongol Kalmuks.

28. See *Mura (Legacy)*, 1, 1986, pp. 50-51.

29. Anonymous. *Zhigitke Öner De Öner Öleng De Öner*, pp. 353-357. Urumqi: Peoples Publishing House of Xinjiang, 1989.

30. Gifts are normally given by the bridegroom's side to the guests and friends from the bride's side.

31. Anonymous. *Zhigitke Öner De Öner Öleng De Öner*, p. 394. Urumqi: Peoples Publishing House of Xinjiang, 1989.

32. A salt water lake in the Ile region, near Yining (Khulzha) city.

33. A *mu* is a Chinese measure for a unit of land, measuring 1/15 of a hectare.

34. A *khulash* is the distance attained between outstretched arms.

35. *Zhanaza* is the ceremony held for the dead; more specifically, the name refers to Qur'anic prayers recited for the dead.

36. Folk Literature and Art Society of China, Xinjiang Branch.

37. Anonymous. *Kazakh Ädebijet Tarihy*, 1, pp. 140-142. Alma Ata: Kazakh SSR Ghylym Akademijasynyng Baspasy, 1960.

Chapter 4

Birth, Horsemanship, and and Circumcision

Poems are recited and songs are chanted to celebrate the arrival of new Kazakh life. The famous poet of Kazakh realism, Abai Khunanbai (1845-1904), has said: "Poems and songs bring one into life; they also send one to the grave." His words refer to the fact that poems and songs express all sentiments of Kazakh life and assist in all its rites of passage.

To commemorate earlier phases in the lives of individuals together with the lives of one's ancestors, to assist young people passing from one phase of life into the next, and to express happiness or sorrow, Kazakh people recite poems and sing songs. Our attempt to sketch the entire span of Kazakh life, from cradle to the grave, begins therefore with poetic creations that pertain specifically to giving birth.

Conception and pregnancy happen ordinarily, in due course, more or less as silent blessings from Allah. But in former times, if a wife has been infertile, she could visit an Immortal.[1] For example, deep in the

Altai mountains is a place named "Toitughysh," a place that features a variety of mineral springs to which healing powers are attributed. Next to these springs is a mountain cave. The people call it "the Cave of Torghaity," the home of the immortal Great One, who lives there the year around. If an infertile woman stays in that cave for the duration of a night she might become pregnant. The Great One who lives there is known to ride forth on a bear and appear here and there—to drop in on a family for a visit. In his hand he carries a magic wand. If with this wand he touches a woman in labor, her child will be born speedily.

The Birth Ceremony *(Shildehana)*

In Kazakh language the rite of giving birth is called *shildehana*. This rite of passage requires staying awake the entire night when a child is being born. Kazakh people consider a newborn child to belong not only to its parents, but to the entire community or *awyl* as well.[2] The birth of a child increases the number and strength of the whole settlement. All the while, not all births are equal. Kazakh people devote special attention to the birth of a boy, and the parents of a boy make no secret of the fact that they are proud.

When a woman begins labor, those who are present hand her the end of a rope to grasp. She takes hold of this rope with both her hands. She leans back and squats low. Several times she groans prayer words such as these: "Immortal Fatima, bless and protect me!"[3]

If midwives are present, the woman in labor will lead them in singing songs like this:

Yes Allah! I beg you to protect and bless me!
Fatima, Angel![4] I petition your help!
Today's singing concerns not only our family,
From ancient times this tradition has been inherited.
Allah is with us and nothing will go wrong,
We do not fear that the child may come crosswise.
The baby shall see the light,
The light, the brilliance of the world.
Here give me strength, Allah!
Yes, my angel Fatima![5]

Many types of songs may be chanted by a woman in labor, but their contents are approximately the same. The main point is always to ask for Allah's blessings and to implore the immortal Fatima for help. The specific hope expressed is that the child may arrive quickly and safely.

As soon as a baby has been born, the husband of the mother is expected to butcher a sheep. This sheep is called the *khalzha*, and the name specifically refers to a sheep butchered for a woman who gives birth. The name *khalzha* also refers to the meat that is prepared on her behalf.

Thereupon follows the actual observance of *shildehana*. Some women remain with the one in childbed for the duration of one to three nights. All the while they eat *khalzha* meat. They sing songs to the accompaniment of a dombra. For the new-born child they wish a long life.

Occasionally the newborn baby, especially the baby of a woman who previously has given birth to children who died, is passed between the thighs of seven other women. In this manner it is given a better chance to survive. Traditionally the death of a child has been associated directly with the identity or condition of its mother. But after a newborn child has been passed through the thighs of seven other women, Death *(Azhal)* can no longer identify the child's real mother. Thus, with Death having become disoriented, the child may be spared. Inherited curses can be evaded in this manner.

On the first night of *shildehana* only women are present. Men of the same age as the child's father join the celebration on the second and third night. So the men and the women, polarized into groups, alternate while singing antiphonal dialogue. The themes of their songs are greetings and good wishes for the well-being of the family, and long life for the newborn child.

The Cradle Ceremony (*Besiktoi*)

In Kazakh tradition there is an event referred to as the Forty Days Ceremony. Literally, *besik toi* means "cradle ceremony." It is celebrated to congratulate a baby's completion of its first forty days. This marks the day when a baby is left to sleep in a cradle by itself.[6] The parents of the baby invite neighboring women to attend this ceremony.

The visitors bring gifts, such as clothes, owl feathers, strings of beads, buttons, or straps for tying the baby into the cradle. They also bring *khalzha* meat and clothes for the baby's mother.

During the Forty Days Ceremony the child will be named. The person who at that ceremony speaks the baby's name should, preferably, be an esteemed old man or a *molda* (mullah) of high status. But when such a personage is not available, names may also be given by parents or by a more common elder or mullah. In any case, the names of many Kazakh boys express the wishes of their parents. Some are named *Bai* (rich man), *Batyr* (hero), *Han-khan* (king, or chief), *Sultan*, and the like. Names for girls may be *Gül* (flower), *Khyz* (girl), *Zhamal* (beautiful, or beauty-face), and the like. Of course, there also are exceptions. If the parents of a baby are already old, and if they have not gotten a son, or if the newborn boy's older brothers have died, the name given might be an unpleasant one—such as *Khoishykhara* (black shepherd boy), *Zhaman-khara* (black bad boy), or *Tokhtar* (stop, stay), and the like.

During the naming rite the namegiver stands by the baby's right side and loudly pronounces a name into its right ear, three times. Then an experienced older woman, who herself has given birth to numerous children, lays the baby into the cradle and fastens the straps.

On special occasions the namegiver, instead of pronouncing the baby's name three times, may elect to recite a poem instead. To that effect, a story has been told about a one-hundred-five year-old widower who married again—he eventually died at the ripe old age of 135. In any case, two years after their marriage his second wife gave birth to a boy. In order to celebrate this happy and cheerful event, the man invited a famous *bij* to name his boy.[7] The chief came and sat down at the right side of the boy. He chanted this song:

> Let the child's name be *Khosmurat*,
> Let him grow up and fly with wings.[8]
> His name comes from Heaven,
> This is an ancient degree.[9]
> The child has been given by Allah,
> Human beings cannot accomplish such miracles.
> Many people, a hundred years old, no longer understand life.
> Even to walk becomes difficult for them.
> To a man over a hundred a son has been given,

How holy Allah is!
This joy is for all of us to share.
May the child, too, live to be a hundred.[10]

The boy has been named by way of reciting this poem. Then, as is customary, the parents gave presents to the invited namegiver. The highest gift on such an occasion could be a horse, or a corduroy overcoat—a *shapan*.

Namegiving provides an opportunity to celebrate for approximately three days. The guests are served tea with milk, various kinds of bread, mutton, and when it is available also *khymyz*—fermented mare's milk.

Beginning with the fortieth day, the baby sleeps in a cradle. Because Kazakh herders move often, and because the mother must transport the cradle on her horse, the baby must be securely tied to the cradle. When a baby is placed into a cradle and refuses to sleep, or when rocking the cradle fails to make a difference, the mother may sing a *besik zhyry*, a cradle song. By way of song a Kazakh mother addresses her child with special names of endearment—such as my Pony, my Little Lamb, my Sunshine.

My dear Pony!
I kiss you with my lips.
You are my first baby I get to see.
My Dear, do not cry so much.
Do not make your mother sad.
Äldi äldi äldi-ai.

My dear Pony!
I hope you will grow and grow.
I rub lamb fat on your body for quick growth.[11]
You are going to crawl and walk.
You are going to be a young man.
Äldi äldi äldi-ai.

My dear Pony!
I bring you up with care.
Your tongue will call me *Täte*.[12]
But in front of other people,
Do not call your brother *Äke*.[13]

Äldi äldi äldi-ai.
My dear Pony!
Do not cry, do not be sad.
Do not ask for the breast before it is time.
Your mother has many house chores to do.
How can she always wait on you?
Äldi äldi äldi-ai.[14]

From such cradle songs we learn how a Kazakh mother thinks, feels, and hopes. She wishes that her child will grow up quickly. We also are given wonderful glimpses of a mother's joyous disposition.

The structure of cradle songs, its lines, its number of syllables in a line, its refrain and its tune are all very regular. But then, while a mother sings a cradle song in accordance with this regular tonal structure, she is free to improvise words and meanings. For example, the cradle song which follows here is of an older variety—even though the content of the third stanza has recently been updated.

My dear Pony!
You are an ear of wheat,
You are an arrow, strong as a camel's *zhilik*.[15]
Your body will be as strong as a yurt pole,
You will be a good farmer.
Äldi äldi äldi-ai.

My dear Pony!
When you ride, your horse will fly like the wind.
When you take its reins,
The steed will float like water.
You will be a good horseman.
Äldi äldi äldi-ai.

My dear Pony!
Your mind will be penetrating.
You will mine treasures from under the earth.
You will ride to the moon and sleep there.
You will be a man of knowledge.
Äldi äldi äldi-ai.

In this lullaby recognition has been given, next to farming and horsemanship, also to the accomplishments of mining engineers and modern space explorers. After all, everywhere it is the role of mothers to dream about the success of their sons, to valorize for their offspring the peak achievements of their culture, such as mine shafts and space ships. Cradle songs have so been chanted far and wide by Kazakh mothers. Upon the wings of soft tunes are carried along not only the intimate sentiments of maternal love, but also the Kazakh ethos of optimism and cultural realism.

Growing up into the World of Men and Horses

A ceremony of horsemanship is held for children, usually for boys, when they begin to mount a horse by themselves for the first time in their lives. Kazakh children start riding on horses as soon as they begin walking. But until they are five years old they always ride together with one of their parents, sitting on their lap. When they reach their fifth birthday they generally have sufficient courage to mount a horse by themselves. It is a solemn occasion when a child first dares to ride on a horse alone, and the parents celebrate accordingly. Owl feathers are attached to the boy's head for decoration on that special day. A boy's first horse usually is one or two years old, and he is seated on a special *ashamai* saddle.[16]

He visits his relatives from door to door. Related women greet the boy by giving presents *(shashyw)*, such as hard cheese, sugar cubes, or fried bread.[17] Male relatives give saddle belts, stirrups, straps, whips, and other such items. Some wealthy relatives may give more expensive gifts, such as a horse or a corduroy overcoat.

When their five-year-old son returns home, his parents prepare a dinner that includes tea with milk, and meat. They serve all the people who arrive with the boy to celebrate. Guests will remark how well the boy can ride his horse, and they will give him important safety instructions: "Always tighten the saddle belt, and be gentle with your horse." When feasible, the head of the family will ask some of the guests to recite an appropriate poem. A recitation may go like this:

Put on the small saddle,
Ride the horse that is under you.

Go from yurt to yurt,
Go from one yurt to another.
Old folks will see you come and will smile,
You will be among them.

They give you a horsewhip,
Will let you whip the horse yourself.
While you are swaying on your horse,
People who see you do it will laugh.
It is all happiness and joy,
To your father and mother as well.

It is from curiosity, and for the sake of ease in moving about, that Kazakh children will want to ride a horse very early in life. Their parents, too, hope that they learn how to ride early on. At some point the children begin to assist in herding and driving livestock. A world of nomadic pastoralism, dominated by men and defined by horsemanship, opens up for the Kazakh boy as he grows up.

It is obvious that the riding habits of Kazakh children, along with the people's general celebration of horsemanship, are based in their economy of herding. That is what sustains the people's special orientation, a genuine love and passion for horses. In their folk literature this love is abundantly expressed. A special vocabulary has been developed to express this love and to describe relationships between humankind and horses.

Today there still can be found men who have the reputation of being special "knowers of horses" *(synshy)*. These men can judge a horse's strength and its running speed from what they can discern by looking at the animal's head, teeth, ears, hooves, and thighs. Horses that are mentioned and described in Kazakh folk literature generally have been appraised by a *synshy*.

Horses have names. They are named in accordance with their age and special characteristics, such as Shybar Dönen (Three-year-old Spot), Khubas (Thinface), Shalkhuirykh (Bigtail).[18] Even though none of these names contain a root that means "horse," a Kazakh knows immediately that they refer to horses.

In Kazakh folk literature, ranging all the way from lengthy epics to short proverbs of two or three sentences, horses are spoken of poetically. For instance, in the famous long poem "Zhanyipa" one finds whole sections dedicated to the description of horses. Zhanyipa is a girl. She dresses as a boy and goes hunting on horseback. By the time her black horse is six years old, the horse which she has been feeding since childhood wins the championship in competition with three thousand other horses. Over the course of twenty years, her horse becomes a champion thirty-two times. When the horse is twenty-five years old, Zhanyipa attends a race in which four hundred and fifty horses compete. On that occasion Zhanyipa and her horse come in third. But then she takes a dombra and plays a tune, and after that her horse wins the championship once more. Finally the horse dies. As a memorial for the beloved animal Zhanyipa builds a tomb and recites a eulogy which enables us to look deep into the soul of a Kazakh horse-lover. Only after her relationship with that black horse draws to a close, does Zhanyipa get married.

Types of character among horses, in Kazakh folk literature, vary widely from situation to situation. In myths and tales, and in heroic epics, horses are not only animals or means of transportation. They are persons like humankind, or sometimes even like mighty gods. In other words, a horse may rank somewhere between a deity and an animal; it may be half human and half divine. When a hero encounters difficulties, or when he is unable to make up his mind, his horse may speak, tell him what to do, and how to overcome his obstacle. In such situations a horse functions like a deity—or, to assume the minimum, as a sounding board for the rider's own mind. Typically, while a hero encounters an enemy his horse reveals itself as very powerful. The horse helps defeat the enemy and saves its master. On such occasions the horse is a fellow hero and humanlike person. At other times, when a human hero is merely going out on a routine journey his horse may merely be a beast of burden. In this manner, horses are different beings for different occasions—gods, senior staff officers, helpers in battle, as well as favored means of conveyance and transportation.

Works in Kazakh folk literature do feature fully developed biographies for horses. These stories usually begin with how an animal was born, and then they leap on to how the animal has helped its human master fight enemies. Accordingly, the growing up of a famous battle steed is narrated significantly different from the life stories of other horses. In epics it is the development of greater than average prowess that is emphasized.

For example, in "Khoblandy" the birth of a hero's steed is described as follows:

> The bluish spotted mare cries pitifully,
> While foam spits forth from her mouth.
> Milk runs from her teats like fountains,
> While she is about to give birth to a colt.
> The future stallion is difficult to be born,
> And the mare walks greatly distressed.
> Suddenly she lies on the ground,
> Tossing from side to side, she suffers great pain.[19]

The difficult labor of the mare, and her master's anxiety, together communicate the point that the colt which is being born is destined to be a special and very fine animal. As might well be expected, the colt which is being born is tall of stature. It is alert and spirited. As soon as it touches the ground it attempts to run and to jump. After wrapping the young animal into his own clothes, its human master carries it away and nurtures it, separate from all the others, until it is five to six years old—and to the end:

> That the sun would not burn him,
> That the rains would not soak him,
> A tent is pitched over him.
> For forty days
> His master feeds him with new mare's milk.[20]
> And for the next forty days
> His master feeds him with milk of a *khysyr*.[21]

As a result of these feedings the filly grows up quickly and healthy. The time comes for the young horse to repay its master for his care. During battles the horse plays three roles. It functions as a deity, as a heroic partner of the human hero, and for contrast and realism's sake occasionally also as an ordinary horse.

In romantic epics, and in love poems, horses have additional characteristics. On one hand they are companions of their owners while, also, they are show animals that for their owners attract someone else's attention. They are of strong and beautiful physique, good natured, and they walk with dignified deportment. Of course, all of these finer aspects in the poet's ornamentation of horses express the intimate dimension to which only lovers can aspire. Still, there are clear situational distinctions. Whereas the battlefield is a place for fierce struggle and requires heroic demeanor on the part of men and horses, an adventure of falling in love calls for profiles of grace and beauty.

Why do Kazakh people love horses? Their answers to this question do vary. Horses have characteristics which humankind especially love and admire. For example, a stallion is known not to mate with his near relatives. If its human master falls to the ground, the horse will not step on him. A horse knows its master and resists a stranger. Horses do not eat dirty grass or drink bad water. And then, from among the four kinds of livestock which Kazakhs keep—sheep, cow, camel, and horse—the spirited nature of horses is most conspicuous. They stride about with aristocratic poise, and they run fast. Finally and foremostly, in the political, the economical, and the cultural life of the Kazakh people, who are nomadic herders on Central Asian steppes, horses play very basic and supportive roles.

The Rite of Circumcision *(Sündet toi)*

The rite of circumcision is practiced by Kazakhs as it is by most other Islamic people. It is a religious rite of initiation, and as such it links together and identifies as Muslims all males who have undergone it. It differentiates them from foreign pagans. All the while, initiation by circumcision among the Kazakh Muslims does have some unique dimensions.

According to Kazakh Islamic custom, boys who are five to seven years old should be circumcised. They generally perform this rite during odd-numbered years.

Before the rite gets under way, the parents of a boy stitch owl feathers to his clothing at his shoulders, and also to his cap. So decorated, the boy rides on a horse to visit his relatives. Female relatives scatter *shashyw* for him, according to their means, and establish a relationship between themselves and the boy. Relatives give him owl feathers, and perhaps a lamb, a calf, or a pony. They also tie some strips of white cloth to the tail of his horse, as a sign that the boy is about to undergo his rite of initiation. During the ceremony some markings are cut into the ear of the pony which had been given to the boy.[22] It signifies that it belongs to him. As the pony grows up it is referred to as the boy's *sündet* horse.

Traditionally circumcision has been done by a mullah or by a special *khozha*, a man who mastered this skill. Special instruments and medicines were used. Before taking hold of the knife and the wooden clamp, a mullah recited a prayer. Then, to stop bleeding the practitioner dusted on some cotton ash. Finally, to protect the wound against friction by fabrics a small bowl formerly was attached to cover the penis. After a few days the little bowl was removed and sheep fat rubbed on the wound.

Nowadays Kazakh parents bring their boys to hospitals and ask Muslim doctors to circumcise them. Any *khozha* or professional physician who performs circumcision nevertheless functions as a religious dignitary. He generally is held in high status.

Before the rite of circumcision begins, sometimes an older parent or grandfather recites a poem to comfort the boy and to explain the rationale of the proceedings:

> This is a tradition.
> It has been handed down by our forefathers.
> It is the mark of being a Muslim.
> It is our father's and mother's duty
> To celebrate this great ceremony.
> It is done to respect our customs, our tradition.
> You are a servant of Allah.
> You are the son of a Muslim.
> It is a good deed *(sawap)* in Allah's sight,
> What your father and mother are doing.[23]
> The way has been instituted by Nurmuhamet,[24]
> For us it is a sacred duty.
> When we arrive in the other world,
> It will be the mark of a Muslim.
> Please Mullah, proceed with your *irim!*[25]
> We have everything ready.

With a lot of explaining the boy is made fully familiar with the reasons for his circumcision. He shores up his resolution and thereby fortifies himself against the pain. It is customary after the rite of circumcision for the boy's parents to sponsor a meal of celebration.

Notes

1. An "immortal" is an *äwlije*—a celestial or supernatural being, a god, deity, or divinity.
2. An average *awyl* is a settlement of four to five interrelated families of the same *ruw* (clan, tribe). The Kazakh language makes no distinction between tribe or clan. For instance, Naiman is a big *ruw* (tribe) which consists of other *ruw* (clans) like Muren and Tölegetai.
3. Fatima *(Patima)*, the Immortal One, Muhammad's daughter and Ali's wife.
4. The Kazakh word for "angel" is *piri*, a Persian word, which also means "beautiful lady." In the Chinese context it means "female celestial being." Kazakhs consider the wives of Muhammad to be *piri*.
5. Folk Literature and Art Society of China, Xinjiang Branch.
6. In Kazakh and in other Turkic languages the number "40" is deemed sacred; it signifies completeness or fullness.
7. A *bii* is head of a hundred families.
8. *Khosmurat*—a "double inheritance" or "hope."
9. This signifies that the child's name is provided by Allah himself.
10. Collected in August 1988 from Beisenghalyi, age 68, in Dörbezhin county of the Tarbaghatai prefecture.
11. Refers to sheep fat which is applied to the child's body for protection against rheumatism and other ailments.
12. A child addresses its sister, sister-in-law, or aunt as *Täte*; also, a firstborn who has been given to its paternal grandparents should address its natural mother as *Täte*.
13. *Äke* does mean Father. But, according to Kazakh custom, the parents are expected to give over their firstborn child to its paternal grandfather and grandmother. Thus, after having formally become the child of its grandparents, and after having suckled the same breast as has its father, this descendant is taught to address its grandfather and grandmother with Father *(Äke)* and Mother *(Apa)*. Its own natural parents, however, must be addressed as Brother *(Agha)* and Sister-in-Law *(Täte)*.
14. This, as well as the next two songs, was obtained from the files of the People's Publishing House of Xinjiang, Urumqi.
15. *Zhilik* is a general designation for the twelve long bones in the limbs of sheep, cows, horses, and camels. Here it refers to a camel's lower leg.

16. A special saddle made for children, in the shape of an "X." At every side the saddle is equipped with safety devices. Decorative painted patterns make it beautiful and showy.

17. *Shashyw* is a general name for all kinds of foods suited for celebrating this joyous occasion—biscuits, cheese, sweets, and *bawyrsakh* (small pieces of deep-fried bread). As a verb, *shashyw* means to scatter. Traditionally, when a hero returned from battle or an ordinary man from a long journey, as from a pilgrimage to Mecca, or when a bridegroom visits his in-laws and the bride arrives at her new home, such foodstuffs are scattered in celebration for anyone to pick up and eat.

18. Kazakhs consider thin-faced horses, those that have little flesh on their heads, to be good horses.

19. "Khoblandy" or "Khoblandy Batyr" is an epic of the 10th to the 12th century. The title bears the name of the epic's primary warrior and hero. See Khazymbek Arabyin, ed. *Kazakh Hyisalary* (*Kazakh Epics*), II, pp. 718-719. Beijing: Nationality Publishing House, 1984.

20. The new milk of a mare that has just given birth is deemed most healthy for a foal.

21. See Khazymbek Arabyin, ed. *Kazakh Hyisalary* (*Kazakh Epics*), II, pp. 718-719. Beijing: Nationality Publishing House, 1984. A *khysyr* is a mare that has not had a colt during the present year; one that has not dried up in the course of the year.

22. Family or clan markings on animals are cut whenever necessary—not only in connection with the celebration of circumcision—into the ears of young "grandson" animals, such as ponies, calves and lambs. These markings may consist of a vertical cut from the middle of the ear to the top *(tilik en)*, a half-round hole cut in the middle of the ear *(ojyk en)*, or a cut sideways *(khyjykh en)*.

23. *Sawap* refers to a good deed, written up as credit, for life in the next world.

24. *Nur* means light, rays of light, brilliant rays, glory—thus the name could be translated with "Glorious Muhammad."

25. To start *irim* means to proceed with the rite prescribed by tradition.

Chapter 5

The Poetry of Marriage

The most common type of marriage arrangement made by Kazakh people is patrilocal, and nowadays it is also monogamous. When a woman marries she goes, in most cases, to live in her husband's home. Prior to 1949, Kazakh society still knew the practice of polygamy. Inasmuch as the dominant religion of the Kazakhs is Islam, it was religiously permissible to marry as many as four wives. Nevertheless, the practice of polygamy generally was limited to families that had wealth, such as the households of aristocrats, of tribal heads and large herd owners. Polygamy was permitted among commoners as well, but for economic reasons its practice was rare.

Traditional Kazakhs arrange the marriages of their offspring in accordance with the ancient rules. Two families of the same clan are not permitted to become related by marriage. For example, the Kerei tribe consists of twelve exogamic clans, a man in any of these clans should marry a wife from one of the eleven others.

Exceptions to the rule of exogamy have been acknowledged in Kazakh tradition. Nevertheless, these exceptions are encumbered with such enormous stipulations that a situation for them almost never arises. If a male and a female of the same clan wish to marry, their actual relatedness should be seven generations apart and their families should have been separated by seven rivers. This immense geographical distance is stipulated for additional separation, because people who live nearby could easily have become formally interrelated in a clan. The chance of "formal interrelatedness" among people who live nearby is increased by the fact that Kazakh women permit other children to suckle their breasts. Babies who drink from the same breast do, by "formal" reckoning, become brothers and sisters. Breastfed stepbrothers and stepsisters become clan members and may not marry any of their brothers or sisters who are on the family's central blood line. As a final safeguard, an endogamic marriage would require the consent of the entire clan.[1]

While sons grow up, their parents will visit neighboring clans to inquire whether there are any suitable girls. After they have chosen—and assuming that the family of the girl will consent—parents of the boy, their relatives or friends, will act as go-betweens. Traditional Kazakh people took great care that a marriage between two families was well matched with regard to social status and the economic wherewithals. The family of a boy would not propose to a girl's family that had higher social status. Even if such a family would have consented, they could not have paid the expected dowry.

Amidst economic balancing, attention was also given to character. There is a saying among Kazakhs: "The mother is a shadow of her daughter." This implies that if the mother is a good woman, her daughter will be good as well. Therefore, girls are chosen with one eye being kept on them while the other eye appraises their mothers.

Some marriages are arranged between families of different clans on an exchange basis, to avoid the dowry payments. Marriages may be arranged involving the offspring of one's mother's brother or sister which, because Kazakh clan membership is patrilineal, naturally belong to a different clan. In fact, a nephew may be given first choice to marry a daughter of his maternal uncle—thus, a cousin. Moreover, two brothers of one clan may marry two sisters of another. Such marriages are sometimes preferred because they tend to be more affordable. If the bride's family were to ask much of a dowry from the family of a groom whose brother has already married an older sister of the bride, they would, in fact, be inflicting a financial hardship on the family to which their older daughter already belongs.

And speaking about affordability and economics, marriages of exchange may be arranged between two families that have both a boy and a girl. By this method they can lighten for themselves the burden of paying dowries. Poor Kazakh nomads usually choose this kind of an even exchange arrangement.

Then also, by special arrangement, if no male heir is present at the home of the bride, if a family has only a daughter, her groom may move to her home—though, this happens seldom in the land of the Kazakhs. A male who moves in with his bride's family is nicknamed a *küshik küyew* (Puppy Son-in-law). At any rate, a puppy son-in-law solves the problem of male labor and succession. His presence is understood as a necessity. While his nickname implies a measure of teasing, in actuality he is not discriminated against.

Kazakh wedding feasts are unique, and they differ significantly from those held by other Chinese nationalities. They are unique from the outset, from matchmaking to the finish.

Altogether there are four wedding rites or *toi* celebrated in the bride's home; these are matchmaking, engagement, presentation of betrothal gifts to the family of the bride, followed by the actual wedding. Two additional rites are then performed in the groom's home; they include another round of gift-giving and the welcoming ceremony. The complexity of all these rites depends on the wealth of the two families.

Matchmaking *(Zhawshy Bolyw)*

Traditionally three basic ways of matchmaking have been followed by the Kazakhs. First, the parents could arrange the marriage of their son entirely on their own initiative. Prior to their efforts the son neither knew about his future in-laws nor came to an understanding with them. He was completely dependent on the will of his parents.

But indeed, there was an alternative to this stern approach. If a boy took a liking toward a girl, he could confide his desire to his sister-in-law, to some other relative, or to a friend. He would ask one of these persons to inform his parents who could then evaluate this matter that weighed on their son's mind. They could themselves go to the girl's home or send a relative to mediate.

A similar, third possibility scenario unfolded if the boy and girl somehow had already fallen in love. In such a case the boy was expected to let his parents know in a proper roundabout way, to the effect that they would visit the girl's home and offer presents. The boy would not go along on that visit. If the parents of the girl agreed, they would accept the gifts and invite their guests to dinner. While both sides were happily celebrating, and were obviously pleased, they decided on a date for the ritual of betrothal or engagement.

Prior to 1949 most Kazakh marriages were arranged by the parents in accordance with one of these three modes. Nowadays some couples exercise full freedom in choosing each other.

Engagement *(Öltiri Toi)*

The engagement or betrothal ceremony is an important step in the process of getting married. The Kazakhs call it *öltiri toi*.[2] It is celebrated at the home of the bride. On a day, which is agreed on by both sides, the parents and close relatives of the groom lead a horse loaded with gifts to the home of the bride. At the female side relatives and friends have been invited as well. As the parents of the girl accept the gifts the marriage arrangement is confirmed.

On that day the girl's family should slaughter a sheep to host their guests. They select a white-headed sheep with some brown or yellow wool on its body. Never must it be a sheep with black wool.

After dinner the head of the girl's household will bring out a large bowl of boiled sheep-tail fat, cut into small pieces and mixed with sheep liver and sour milk. The guests cannot eat this food with their own hands. It must be fed directly into the mouth of every guest by women from the girl's side. A guest must participate willingly and be well behaved. Otherwise the women will dump the mixture on the guest's face, in jest.

When the people of the bridegroom return home, the head of the girl's family sends along some gifts as well—such as fabrics for clothing. If they are wealthy they may give horses as well, or other expensive gifts. From that day on the two families remain in close contact. The male side continues to send livestock to the family of the bride, the number that had been agreed to by both sides.

The Presentation of Betrothal Gifts *(Zhyrtys Toi)*

Zhyrt means "to tear," and "zhyrtys" is the noun which describes an event of tearing. In ancient days, when someone was buried, pieces of cloth were brought out and torn into segments for the funeral attendants. Such a "tearing event" also takes place when a future son-in-law comes to the bride's home for the first time. He is expected to bring along a preliminary engagement gift—including some meters of cloth which are then torn and divided, in unequal portions, among his future sister-in-laws.

Nowadays the tearing rite is done a few days before the actual wedding. On the day when these proceedings take place, the groom's family invites relatives and friends to their yurt. They display all the *zhyrtys* articles for people to inspect and to admire. The people examine these gifts as to whether they appear finished or not, or whether their quality is good enough. Relatives and friends of the groom will bring along some additional gifts, as a precaution against the possibility that some of the other gifts may not pass inspection. In accordance with Kazakh tradition, all relatives and friends will do their best.

The traditional delivery of betrothal gifts is also known as "Visiting Ceremony." It is celebrated at the home of the bride after the *zhyrtys* or "tearing." To begin with, the groom's side informs the bride's side that all is ready to deliver the gifts. Then the female side will choose a favorable or lucky day which, in accordance with tradition, usually happens to be a Wednesday *(Sarsenbi küni)*. In Kazakh this name literally means "propitious day."

On the chosen day the bridegroom and a friend will ride on horseback to deliver their gifts to the yurt of the bride. Parents and close relatives, such as aunts, sisters and brothers of his mother, will accompany them. Upon having approached the yurt of the bride to about five to three hundred meters, the groom dismounts from his horse and lingers. He will not approach together with his friend and his relatives. Instead, young people from the settlement come out to welcome him and to lead his horse with its load of gifts. On arrival at the bride's yurt they quickly disappear into their own homes.

Meanwhile the parents of the bride, and other relatives, stand outside their yurt to welcome the guests. The sister-in-law of the bride, together with a group of young women and girls, will go to welcome the groom. While he approaches, an old and highly respected woman scatters *shashew* for him and speaks the greeting. They bring the groom to a small yurt that has been especially prepared for his reception. On that day the girl's family welcomes the guests and slaughters some sheep for the feast. They play on dombras, dance together, and celebrate cheerfully.

On the second day, after breakfast, two or three women from the bride's side unwrap the gifts. They show them to their relatives and friends for inspection. If they are not in finished form they will ask that they be completed.

On that same day, additional gifts should be brought to the parents of the bride, and also to her brothers and sisters. This quiet round of giving must include, specifically, some kind of sheep or cow, or some other animal, for the mother of the bride—for having suckled the bride when she was still a baby. This practice is called *uryn baryw toi* (go quietly ritual), or *esik köriw toi* (door finding ritual). The latter may be explained as a "ritual for getting to know the house-door."[3]

At night the bridegroom sleeps in a yurt all by himself. Then at midnight, when everybody is asleep, the bride accompanied by her sister-in-law will come to the groom's yurt to consummate their marriage. The groom is expected to give generous gifts to the sister-in-law of his bride—thanking her for having helped them sleep together for the first time and to get married. These proceedings are an old custom among Kazakhs; they are referred to as "first wedding." After that night, and before the bride moves to her husband's yurt, the groom may enter his father-in-law's yurt at any time. He now belongs.

The Getting Married Ceremony *(Khyz Uzatyw Toi)*

Inasmuch as the nomadic Kazakhs range over vast areas, it is typical that not long after the delivery of betrothal gifts the bride will be moving far away from her native place—to live with the groom's family.

The Getting Married Ceremony, which Kazakhs call *khyz uzatyw toi,* is a grandiose event. It is ordinarily held during autumn, which is a convenient time for the bridegroom's side to deliver livestock to the parents of the bride. The festivities which follow that delivery last three days, and during these days the people on the female side invite all their relatives, and additional people of their clan. These days provide an opportunity for the entire clan to stage games of horsemanship, such as *lakh tartew* and *khez kuwar,* and to hold *akhyn aitys.*

Adult games of horsemanship, like *lakh tartyw* (kid grabbing), are performed throughout Central Asia. Here it is done with the headless disembowelled carcass of a goat kid, elsewhere it may be done with a headless calf. Ten to thirty horsemen line up at each side. The carcass must be picked up from horseback, from within a central circle, and carried home under the rider's thigh. The opposing side tries to snatch it away to win it for themselves. The side which brings the carcass safely to their yurt, has won the game.

The kid-grabbing game, *lakh tartyw,* is also named *kökpar tartyw* (wolf-grabbing).[4] It may be assumed that this game originated with a victory celebration over a wolf that was killed. Wolves were considered enemies by nomadic Kazakh herders, and the contestants vied with one another to victoriously bring home the dead wolf. Inasmuch as all the serious games of *Homo ludens sapiens* degenerate into sports for sports sake, the carcass of a convenient herd animal was substituted.[5]

Khez khuwar is a game on horseback played by boys and girls. The playground is 300 to 400 meters long. The race begins at one end where the girls are given a ten to fifteen meter lead; the odds are further slanted against the boys in that the girls are usually given better horses to ride on. The boys give chase to catch up and to kiss a girl during the chase—and the latter are not expected to resist that fate. However, once the goal mark at the end of the track has been reached and circled, the girls may chase the boys with whips. They are permitted to hit hard. If the boys were lucky enough to escape without being hit, they could count such success as a victory.[6]

On the day before the feast the bride's side slaughters some sheep and makes preparations for the arrival of guests. Parents of the bride set up a small yurt in which to store the dowries. The parents may invite a well respected man from among their clan to speak for them, to convey congratulations to their daughter. Their expressed good wishes include that she may go to her new family, to the groom's family, to be a diligent and kind woman. From that day on the bride is expected to remain inside her yurt in the company of a group of girls. Her face should remain covered with a veil.

The Wedding Songs *(Saryn)*

On the first day of the wedding, relatives and friends of the bride sing songs to a special tune. The purpose of their singing is to praise the groom and thereby, teasingly, persuade the bride not be overly sad—because the fate of getting married is inevitable. Here is an example of such a song:

In the name of Allah, let me sing about your bridegroom, üki-aw!
Please listen carefully, and be not sorrowful, üki-aw!
To get married in the course of one's life is inevitable, üki-aw!
Such wedding songs your ancestors have sung before, üki-aw.[7]

We have noted the melody for another one of these *saryn* songs. Its words make it obvious that comfort is being offered not only for consolation, but also to generate emotion and to draw tears.

Saryn starts with *bismillä* (in the name of God), üki-aw.
Bismillä comes once in a thousand years, üki-aw.
Please let me speak my mind, my Dear! üki-aw.
Do not cry, but listen attentively! üki-aw.

I sing the *saryn* to my child, üki-aw.
Do not let my breath be in vain, üki-aw.
These are our customs left from of old, üki-aw.
Who would dare to go against our tradition, üki-aw.

Let me sing the *saryn* to you, üki-aw.
Let me sing it to you without hesitation, üki-aw.
When you are married, be polite, üki-aw.
Do not disgrace yourself, my Dear! üki-aw.

Your father holds this ceremony for you, üki-aw.
For the ceremony he slaughtered lots of animals, üki-aw.
You are a child whom everyone treats with respect, üki-aw.
You will be married and we feel grieved, üki-aw.

You will cry and call your dad, my Dear, üki-aw.
"My faults are so many," you say, üki-aw.
Your father never mentioned any before, üki-aw.
"When she grows up I will exchange her for cattle," üki-aw.

Do not cry or bathe your face in tears, üki-aw.
What young people do not enjoy having fun, üki-aw.
"I will not give you in marriage," said your dad, üki-aw.
Would they who gave the cattle let you off? üki-aw.

You will cry and call your mother, my Dear, üki-aw.
"I am helpless being young," you say, üki-aw.
When she brings you to your husband, üki-aw.
"How can I stay here and cry?" you say, üki-aw.

You will cry and call your brother, my Dear, üki-aw.
"I am completely useless when I think about you," üki-aw.
You will not stop crying and sobbing, üki-aw.
"How can I adapt to a strange place?" üki-aw.

You will cry and call your younger brother, my Dear, üki-aw.
"Joyful days we have spent together," you say, üki-aw.
Your longing will never disappear, üki-aw.
"My faults will be exposed there," you say, üki-aw.

Oh, do not cry and call on your sister-in-law! üki-aw.
"Just like gold buttons on my breast," you say, üki-aw.[8]
Oh dear girl! Please do not cry, üki-aw.
Please do not think "Now I am in a strange place," üki-aw.

You are riding on the back of a white horse, üki-aw.
Your coat is made of brocade, üki-aw.
"I will not give you in marriage," your dad said, üki-aw.
But God has created you for a strange place, üki-aw.

You cry and miss your native home, üki-aw.
When you think of it you are deeply grieved, üki-aw.
You will always daydream about it, üki-aw.
You will always miss your native home, üki-aw.

You put up a white yurt on the flat, üki-aw,
Villagers come and congratulate you, üki-aw.
If you do not want to be married, üki-aw,
Why not say "Don't marry me!" üki-aw.

You put up a white yurt at the hillside, üki-aw.
Women come there for eating (festival) meat, üki-aw.
If you do not want to be married, üki-aw,
Why not throw them all out? üki-aw.

Outside your door is a dense forest, üki-aw.
In there you have herded your sheep, üki-aw.
This is a lively wedding feast, üki-aw.
Sing and dance, lads and chaps, üki-aw.

Farewell, my Dear, upon your going away, üki-aw,
Do not cry on account of anything, my Dear, üki-aw.
Even if you have much wealth, üki-aw,
Nothing can compare with this joyful scene, üki-aw.

Inasmuch as you were born, you are a girl, üki-aw.
You are from a noble family, üki-aw.
We wish the swan flies over your head, üki-aw.
God be with you and you be happy, üki-aw.

Inasmuch as you were born, everybody likes you, üki-aw.
What your fancies are, strangers do not understand, üki-aw.
We wish the swan flies over your head, üki-aw.
God be with you, and you be happy! üki-aw.

You are riding on the back of a black horse, üki-aw.
The horse was trained by a man, üki-aw.
Even though we say "We will not marry you off," üki-aw,
Those who gave the cattle, would not agree, üki-aw.

Your are riding on the back of a yellow horse, üki-aw.
If you do not ride this horse it feels concern, üki-aw.
Until you leave your native place, üki-aw,
Your sobs and tears will not cease, üki-aw.

O dear girl, you are gentle and soft as wheat straw, üki-aw.
Do not be arrogant and a nuisance, üki-aw.
Both of you were born to be a pair, üki-aw.
Just like Sapymülik and Zhamal, üki-aw.

Zylyigha and Jüsip united together, üki-aw.[9]
Who would dare to go against our tradition, üki-aw.
No matter who sheds tears, we do not mind, üki-aw.
While parting we cannot stop the flow of tears, üki-aw.

Gather up your courage and do not cry, my Dear, üki-aw.
All of us are with you, üki-aw.
The Prophet, too, married his girl, üki-aw.
He covered her face with a white veil, üki-aw.

Khadyja and Aisha are your two sisters, üki-aw.
They did not (continue to) enjoy happiness and gaiety, üki-aw.
They remained not at their parental home forever, üki-aw.
They did not (continue to) enjoy happiness and gaiety, üki-aw.

When the *saryn* begins it is clear, üki-aw,
That you are a girl gentle and meek, üki-aw.
I wish you good luck in that new place, üki-aw.
The place to which you are going is foreign to you, üki-aw.

You wear a red garment on you, üki-aw.
Embroidered flowers on your sleeves and breast, üki-aw.
The first woman of whom we know was Eve, üki-aw,
She also got married to a man, üki-aw.

Are your two camels twins or a pair? üki-aw.
Is the dowry-carrying dromedary fat and strong? üki-aw.
Do not trouble their hearts with your words, üki-aw.
Do not let them dislike their only girl, üki-aw.

The coat you wear is made of brocade, üki-aw.
Do not cry so grievously, O my Dear! üki-aw.
Do not be a baby eagle, weak and incompetent, üki-aw.
Do not leave behind a bad reputation, üki-aw.

One of you is honey, and the other is sweet, üki-aw.
You (two) are just like a new moon, üki-aw.
God has joined both of you together, üki-aw.
Be a devoted couple to the end of you lives, üki-aw.[10]

Sweetheart Songs *(Zhar-zhar)*

While the bride listens to *saryn* songs, concealed behind a curtain, she inevitably begins to cry. The young men, friends and relatives, who sang the *saryn* verses dismount from their horses and accompany the approaching groom to the yurt of the bride. One of them rolls up the piece of felt which serves as door to the yurt. The people inside and outside can now see each other, and they begin to sing the sweetheart songs *(zhar-zhar)*. *Zhar* means "sweetheart," and a double *zhar* constitutes the refrain of this type of songs. The tunes of the sweetheart songs are happy and tranquil; their content is humorous and witty.

The people sing in antiphonal or dialogue style. The young men start with asking provocative questions while the girls, inside the yurt, sing the answers together with the bride. Young men sing about the joy of being married, and girls sing about their anxiety. Naturally, not all concerns that can be raised in such songs are found in one sample. In any case, the young men and boys outside may begin like this:

Zharzhar menen bastajyn sözding basyn zhar - zhar. Zhar - zha ry ma khulakh sal

kharyn da sym zhar - zhar. Buryn ghynyng myira sy khyzu za tyw.

zhar - zhar, betal dyngnan biral la zharyl khasyn zhar - zhar.

Let us start our song with *zhar-zhar*, zhar-zhar.
Listen carefully to my *zhar-zhar*, dear younger sister, zhar-zhar.
To marry off a daughter is an old tradition, zhar-zhar.
Be happy, Allah will bless and protect you, zhar-zhar.

Boys singing *zhar-zhar* are clever and eloquent, zhar-zhar.
Are not the joys of life like this? zhar-zhar.
If the loves of two joined together are not pure, zhar-zhar.
There will be no happiness in their lives, zhar-zhar.

You are a white fledgling in the nest, zhar-zhar.
You are an eagle egg under an overhanging cliff, zhar-zhar.
May the place you go be prosperous and beautiful, zhar-zhar.
May it support your parents as well, zhar-zhar.

It is a great happiness to be a pair, zhar-zhar.
Setting up a yurt for yourselves is a good deed, zhar-zhar.
If two who join are equal, that is quite enough, zhar-zhar.[11]
The wedding gifts you took are pure and honest, zhar-zhar.

I am not flattering you with empty words, zhar-zhar.
You have been polite to elders all along, zhar-zhar.

With companions you never grinned tongue in cheek, zhar-zhar.
You are a girl whom everyone applauds, zhar-zhar.

While mentioning you your father and mother weep, zhar-zhar.
Where can they find (another one like) you? zhar-zhar.
When you were born people said "it is a girl," zhar-zhar.
You were born to belong to a strange land, zhar-zhar.

Do not be stingy while entertaining your guests, zhar-zhar.
Because that is forbidden by our ancient tradition, zhar-zhar.
Your parents who brought you up love you dearly, zhar-zhar.
Do not let others say you are weak and unproductive, zhar-zhar.

Knee-cap and angle-bone are in one's leg, zhar-zhar.
The khan has knowledge about everyone, zhar-zhar.
Do not worry about your father who is left at home, zhar-zhar.
If you are a good wife your father-in-law is there too, zhar-zhar.

The response from girls and young ladies, inside, may resound as follows:

Horses at our *awyl* are eating mugwort, zhar-zhar.
Horses that eat mugwort run speedily, zhar-zhar.
I feel indebted to my father, zhar-zhar.
He said "I never marry you off, darling of our home," zhar-zhar.

Lift the knitted bed spread and let mother look at me, zhar-zhar.
Let my mother read blessings for her daughter, zhar-zhar.
Her (mother's) tears are dropping into her own heart, zhar-zhar.
Let mother take the load off her mind, zhar-zhar.

I did not pull the four ropes of the skylight tight, zhar-zhar.[12]
Why, in my home, am I no longer tolerated? zhar-zhar.
I am weeping bitterly, but to no avail, zhar-zhar.
I am reluctant to leave my parents for another place, zhar-zhar.

My veil is waved to and fro by the wind, zhar-zhar.
Who endures my childlike ways, as at home? zhar-zhar.
If I am a good wife, mother-in-law will accept me, zhar-zhar.
If I am a bad wife she will scold severely, cruelly, zhar-zhar.

Young branches thrown in the river float away, zhar-zhar.
Such kindness will never be duplicated again, zhar-zhar.

"A father of others is like your own," people say, zhar-zhar.
Is there anyone who loves me like my own father? zhar-zhar.[13]

Here follow two *zhar-zhar* songs that were recorded in the Tarbaghatai prefecture:

1. Hip-bone and thigh-bone are connected, zhar-zhar.
Kazakh grasslands are close to the mountains, zhar-zhar.
Girls grown up, they should be married off, zhar-zhar.
They should not remain home with father and mother, zhar-zhar.

In spring-time flowers are going to blossom, zhar-zhar.
Girls grown up, they should be married off, zhar-zhar.
After flowers have bloomed they will bear fruit, zhar-zhar.
After girls are married they will soon be mothers, zhar-zhar.

While girls are at home they learn to embroider, zhar-zhar.
When girls get married they ride on fine horses, zhar-zhar.
Getting married to a new *awyl* their veils are removed, zhar-zhar.
The place you go to is a good and honest place, zhar-zhar.

Your father and mother supported you until eighteen, zhar-zhar.
Girls at eighteen should get married, zhar-zhar.
When girls get married they should be happy, zhar-zhar.
No need to be shy, or weep and wail endlessly, zhar-zhar.

Hip-bone and thigh-bone are connected, zhar-zhar.
No one has the strength to move a mountain, zhar-zhar.
Our old tradition is to advise you to get married, zhar-zhar.
Our traditions come from our ancestors, zhar-zhar.

2. Let us set up our snow-white yurt, zhar-zhar.
Let us pile up our new silk bedding, zhar-zhar.
Let us place the saddles adorned with silver, zhar-zhar.
Let us hang up the embroidered flannel blankets, zhar-zhar.

Let us set up the newly made wooden bed, zhar-zhar.
Let us hang up the red bed-curtain, zhar-zhar.

Let us spread the newly made embroidered felt, zhar-zhar,
These are just waiting for the bride to get married, zhar-zhar.

Let us hang up the clear mirror, zhar-zhar.
The bridal chamber is brightened, zhar-zhar.
The purplish red mare is neighing, zhar-zhar.
She welcomed the girl who is getting married, zhar-zhar.

I, the bard *(akhyn),* am now singing, zhar-zhar!
In your new home are good father- and mother-in-law, zhar-zhar.
Do not resent parting from your native place, zhar-zhar.
The life that awaits you is very good, zhar-zhar.[14]

Young Lady Songs *(Bijkem)*

Young fellows who are good at impromptu *zhar-zhar* singing do
their rounds first. Older men who stand by the door, listening, will
then get into the act and add: "Amen, Amen! God bless and protect
you!" Then the bride, the ladies and young girls who are with the
bride, will join the singing as well. They either sing a *zhar-zhar* or a
bijkem song. *Bijke* is the respectful form for referring to a grown-up
girl, thus a young lady. "Young lady songs" are generally patterned
like the following sample:

My red scarf is waiving in the wind, bijkem.
Who understands my disposition and distress? bijkem.
If my mother-in-law is good she will understand me, bijkem.
If not, she will scold me and call me a lazy-bone, bijkem.

Floating willow twigs have no weight, bijkem.
I grew up and was pampered since my childhood, bijkem.
Even though my mother-in-law is also a mother, bijkem,
How can she compare with my mother and father? bijkem.[15]

Songs of Lament *(Syngsyma)*

The bride now removes the cap which is typically worn by girls.
An old lady of good reputation and character will then cover her head

with a veil, instead. This signifies that the bride is now going to leave her home. She begins to weep, and with a soft and mournful voice she sings *syngsyma* songs.[16] It is by way of such songs that the bride will pour out her heart and reveal her innermost feelings of anguish. With the words of these songs a bride bids farewell to her native homestead, and to her loved ones:

Akh o tawym tikken zher oi law bolsen, äi - ow akhzhü zimdi köriw ge

Kisia nasy kisi ge a na dei di. Aina lajyn apam dai

ainam bolsyn, ai-ow.

khaidan bolsyn, ai-ow.

Ei, elim - ow khoshe sen bol zhe rim - aw!

If only my yurt were set up on the flat grassland, ai-ow.
If only there were a mirror for me to look at my face, äi-ai.
People say, the mother of another is like your own, ai-ow.
How can she be as close as my own mother, äi-ai.
Oh you, my native place!
Good-bye to you, place of my birth!

Farewell, dear Mom, be well! ai-ow.
Let me awaken you and arouse your love to me, äi-ai.
Oh my God! Why was I made a girl? ai-ow.
Was it your aim to make me cry? äi-ai.
Oh you, my native place!
Good-bye to you, place of my birth!

Oh, dear Mother, crying with tears, ai-ow.
Where can I find a mother like you? äi-ai.
Not even sixteen years old, you married me off, ai-ow.
Do you not have the strength to stop my father? äi-ai.

Oh you, my native place!
Good-bye to you, place of my birth!

Oh, dear Father, though I am a girl I am like your son, ai-ow.
I am a piece of velvet which you bought at the market, äi-ai.
You forced me to be married, ai-ow.
I am just like a foal, orphaned and helpless, äi-ai.
Oh you, my native place!
Good-bye to you, place of my birth!

If I were a boy, would I not support you, dear Father? ai-ow.
Would I not attend races riding on a flying horse? äi-ai.
As does our native place when blossoms are out, ai-ow.
Would I not make you happy and joyful? äi-ai.
Oh you, my native place!
Good-bye to you, place of my birth!

You forest, swaying before our door, ai-ow.
While I long for you my agony is hard to describe, äi-ai.
The father of another is not the same as one's own, ai-ow.
Who can be compared with you, dear Dad! äi-ai.
Oh you, my native place!
Good-bye to you, place of my birth!

Good-bye, dear Dad. Let me say good-bye, ai-ow.
It is for you that my tears are bathing my face, äi-ai.
O my place of birth! O my kindred! You remain behind, ai-ow.
Today I am saying good-bye to you all, äi-ai.
Oh you, my native place!
Good-bye to you, place of my birth!

Oh dear Brother, I am going far away, ai-ow.
Be fair. Or do I have no longings? äi-ai,
When I step off the threshold of our home, ai-ow.
Come and visit me often, äi-ai.
Oh you, my native place!
Good-bye to you, place of my birth!

We grew up together like foals, dear Brother, ai-ow.
Leisurely carefree times are hard to return to, äi-ai.

I am going to a strange place and am leaving our home, ai-ow.
How can I adapt in a home of others? äi-ai.
Oh you, my native place!
Good-bye to you, place of my birth!

We grew up like lambs and kids, dear younger sisters, ai-ow.
Oh my native *awyl*, you will feel deserted, äi-ai.
Please do not tell why you produce so many tears, ai-ow.
It is difficult to describe the depth of my sorrow, äi-ai.
Oh you, my native place!
Good-bye to you, place of my birth!

I will remember you, my native place, ai-ow.
With me you will lose an ardent lover, äi-ai.
From early youth I played and laughed on your grounds, ai-ow.
If I have faults, please forgive, forgive this pitiful girl, äi-ai.
Oh you, my native place!
Good-bye to you, place of my birth!

I have not drunk enough the clear waters of your springs, ai-ow.
I regret not belonging to you anymore, äi-ai.
O God! You take me away from my home, ai-ow.
Why not take away my soul with me as well, äi-ai.
Oh you, my native place!
Good-bye to you, place of my birth!

Do you hate me, my dear native place? ai-ow.
If you do, please move elsewhere too, äi-ai.
One leaves his home if one is dead, ai-ow.
I leave my home, though I am still alive, äi-ai.
Oh you, my native place!
Good-bye! Salam (Peace) to you! Fare well![17]

Songs of Sorrow (*Köris Ajtyw*)

After the bride has sung *syngsyma* songs she steps before her
parents, brothers, sisters, and other relatives to begin a *köris* song. She
is accompanied by two young ladies. To all her relatives she sings:

Ow,   esikting   aldy   betkeidi-aw,   betkeiden   malym   keitpeidi-aw,

aina   lajyn   el-zhurtym,   khadyryng   esten   ketpeidi-aw.

Outside the door is a broad and level place-*aw*,
Groups of animals are playing on the broad grassland-*aw*,
Dear relatives, my native place,
I will never forget your great kindness-*aw*.

While I was young you (my Mother) pampered me,
While I was young I never felt wronged.
How can I be a woman,
If I depart from your side?

How happy it is to climb to the top of a mountain!
Wild sheep are playing halfway up that mountain.
But, I was a girl when I was born,
And I became a bag that belongs to others.

Snow flakes are falling thick and fast,
It is you, my Mother, who brought me up.
Dear Mother, I remember you with longing,
Oh, I will spend my time with tears.

I do not want to leave you, my dear Mother,
I cannot stop the tears flow from my eyes.
In your heart I am your child,
Why can I not stay with you always?

Along the stream stand white birch trees,
I want to treasure and protect them,
As long as I live,
I will repay you for your kindness.

Is it a pine or a willow?
Are there trees harder than birches?
Although I say "Don't cry" to myself,
Is there anything as pitiful as girls?

The tea table brought from the market,
How can I take care and not ruin it?
Oh! My Mother, you gave me your milk,
What must I do so as not to disappoint you?

To her father she sings:

A yellow sturdy horse stands in the horse herd,
A yellow horsewhip lies heavy in your hand.
Had I been born a boy,
I would stay with you in the *awyl*. Would I not?

Oh! Outside the door are thorn bushes,
Oh! Do you know how sorrowful I am?
Father! Please do not send me away.
Let me stay with you for another year!

There is a gray racing stallion in the herd,
Nobody can catch him with bare hands.
You are going to send me far away,
How pitiful I am, and what can I do?

Today I wear a white skirt,
I comb my hair and wear it in braids.
O Father, you said you would not marry me off,
Why do you become so cruel-hearted?

To her brother she sings:

Dear Brother, please listen to me,
The seat you are sitting on is a throne.
Although we were born into the same family,
We cannot always remain together.

My dear Brother,
I have put the horses out to the pasture.

Customs of strange lands I do not know.
How could I know their tempers?

I wish I were a white swan,
I wish I could dwell at the lake side.
Do not cry, Brother, do not cry.
I hope to support your song ever after.

There is a brownish mare in the herd,
Riding on her back you drive our cattle.
Come to me regularly, tarry not too long,
People will say "Her brother is here."

Birds will flap their wings before flying,
Birds will drop into nets carelessly.
O my Brother, you said you will not marry me off.
Why have you, too, been deceived?

To her sister-in-law she sings:

Bismillä is the beginning of our words.
Tears dropping from my eyes do never cease.
I do not want to leave you, oh Sister-in-law!
Are we going to leave each other like this?

I wear on me a white skirt,
Beautiful flowers are embroidered on it.
O dear Sister-in-law, I love you.
You also liked me in a special way.

The Altai range has high mountains.
Ribbons of our fur hats are made of silk.
Although I say to myself "Do not cry,"
God made us women, inferior to others.

To her younger brother she sings:

Dear younger Brother, let me kiss you,
Let me kiss your hair.
How can you remain behind?
We followed each other so closely.

There are corduroys in the market,
You are a good son of our father.
Be a good helper to our father,
These are my words to you, my dear younger brother.

Dear younger Brother, you are like the sun,
My Dear One, you never went and left me alone.
But now the time is approaching,
My breath trembles deeply.

The fierce wind is howling,
A well-known mountain is our Sawyr.
I am going away and you are left,
Peace by with you, my dear younger Brother!

To the threshold she sings:

Before the door grow burdock plants.
Do not let me go away, my Threshold.
How can I stop the tears roll from my eyes,
I am so full of sorrow, half dead.

Larks are flying in the sky,
May the feathers of larks be pure and white.
I cannot avoid having to leave you,
Good-bye now, my dear Threshold.[18]

As she proceeds along her way she sings another *köris* song:

On me I wear a white skirt,
My folks are sending me away.
The place I go to is far, far away,
Oh, I will remember you with longing.

I am riding on a winged steed.
Flowers are embroidered on my riding boots.
My younger brother is left behind me.
When will he grow up and be a young man?

There is a white horse in the horse herd,
Children cannot catch him.
My father is old, my brother is young,
Dear folks, please look after them.

There are twins in the sheep herd,
The ends of rivers are in the ocean.
My *Awyl*, you will no longer call me "Girl,"
From now on you will say "the young wife is coming."[19]

Köris songs are intoned with deep emotion and sorrow; sometimes they run to great lengths. Here is another example:

Oh, my native place and sandy bank,
My Brother, Sister, and Sister-in-law.
When I think about my native place,
My heart feels like stalling.

A willow stands before my door,
What trees are taller than it?
Born at my place, I will grow old on the steppe,
Is there anyone as unfortunate as girls?

Like the marrow in the spine,
My father, you looked after me as if I were a son.
When you were in debt to someone,
You caught me like a foal to send me away.

I tied a horse to the stable,
I boiled honey in a pot.
O my dear Mom,
I have not yet grown up and here you marry me off.

Oh dear Allah! Creator!
The wild horse runs away and is difficult to catch.
Until we meet again, next time,
I say goodbye and wish you all safe and sound.

There is a horse in the herd,
With a yellow neck and lowered head.
My brothers and sisters remain left behind,
I will never again enjoy happiness with them.

Instead of the *börik* (round girls' cap) on my head,
My face is covered with a pink veil.
O dear Mother! O my Dear!
Your yurt will seem hollow and empty.

When I was born I was not a boy,
I have not driven horses down the mountains.
O dear Dad! O my Dear!
[As a girl] I have not saddled your horse for you.

Spring water runs down from the mountain,
The fine hair of a small camel is soft.
While I think about my native place,
All my bones and muscles ache.

I ride on a horse, with a whip in my hands.
Tears run down from my eyes.
Like a hired herdsman,
You drive me off from my native place.

A brownish foal plays in the herd,
People will return from summer pasture soon.
Call on me and visit me often,
Or else they will say "She has none who loves her."

Come call on me and visit me,
Come and give me help.
Before I grow up as a full adult,
Come to me and watch over me.

There is a black foal in the herd,
Pat its back gently.
To part from my native place is not my will,
It will be a long time until we meet again.

Under our luggage is my tea table,
How can I keep from damaging it?
Dear Mother, you brought me up with care,
What can I do not to be unworthy?

I am a lamb in the sheep herd,
I am a foal in the horse herd.
Alongside my parents, Dad and Mom,
I was circling like a swan.

I am a swan henceforth no longer,
But I will never forget my home and my kin.
I never will forget you like the cloud that floats away.
How can I forget you—Brother, Sister-in-law, Relatives!

I tied my luggage onto the camel,
I tied it firm with silk rope.
Goodby my native people and kin,
I am crying and telling you.

A shed stands outside our door,
My horse is frightened by the shed.
Although mother said: "I will not marry you off!"
Now she drapes the veil over my face.

A black rock stands on the mountain top,
An eagle alights on that rock.
I do not want to leave my home,
Must I leave my home like this, just now?

A pine tree stands on the mountain top,
Let the larks perch on that pine.
We are age mates, we grew up together,
I regret we cannot be so close anymore.

A black rock stands on the mountain top,
An eagle alights on that rock.
O my Brother, you said "I will not marry you off!"
Oh, I cannot remain at your side.

Stones are piled up in front of the door,
Girls are useless, just as these stones.
If girls are useful, the same as boys,
Then why am I so useless and not like others?

We ate apples and apricots together,
Sister-in-law you were my companion.
Now I am going far away, my Dear,
Your doomed sister, not yet dead.

Large burdock plants are growing by the door.
Wild horses are difficult to catch.
Until I return to this place again,
You all remain safe and sound!

A bluish saddle was bought at the market,
I sit on it and I feel proud.
While I put my feet into the stirrups,
My feelings are difficult to describe.

Licorice plants grow by the door,
Horses stand around the licorice plants.
You who have helped me ride the horse,
How hard-hearted all of you are!

Why did you, Our God, make us girls?
Why like sheep, for paying family debts?
Girls are made for all the others,
We must act according to the whims of others.

Yesterday the wind was blowing hard,
My *awyl* looks like whipped-up water on the lake.
Now I am leaving, must part from you,
Be safe and sound, all you my brothers.

People are praying in the morning.
Oh, my home looks as lively as a market.
Now I am leaving to part from you.
Oh, where is that place to which I am going?

Many kinds of grasses are growing by our door,
Oh, I drove away three horses.
My older brothers, you said "I will not marry you off!"
And you handed the reins to me today.

I was so happy-go-lucky at home,
I was pampered and spoiled with tea brought to me.
But all my years of pampering have passed,
I feel sorrowful and upset, Mom!

You are not willing to send me away,
Tears from your eyes do not stop.
The pitiful fetus remains in your womb,
Why am I not at your side now, dear Mom?

There are embroideries now on my arms,
Do not cry for me anymore.
While I think about you, my dear Mom,
My heart feels constricted.

I was a girl when I was born,
When God sent me to this earth.
Had I been born a boy,
Would I not remain at your side, dear Brother?

My clothes are sewed with silver buttons,
I have never been beaten by the weather.
I have been so spoiled by my parents,
But what will my future be?

Oh, my hair is soft and long,
I have been so spoiled by my parents.
When I am in a strange place,
Will I be at my wit's end?

I made a chest and covered it with lead,
Patterns I carved upon it.
I entrust my father and my mother
To the one almighty God.

There are carvings on my horsewhip,
When silk is dyed the color does not fade.
No matter how many good people there are,
Nobody is better than one's own mother.

People spend winters near the springs of rivers,
There are velvet decorations on my sleeves.
No matter how many good people there are,
Nobody looks after you like your own mother.

There is a white horse in the horse herd.
"The girl is to be married," spread the word.
"I do not give you to anyone, my Dear," said my father.
Why do changes happen so fast?

A foal of last year became a *tai* (two-year-old) by now.
The new moon rises in the sky.
My brothers also said: "We do not give you to anyone."
But words about giving me away they now speak.

A stream is murmuring by my door,
I bow down to wash my face.
Being a girl, I am going to get married,
Do not be anxious, my dear Mom.

I drove the horse to the market,
People are moving onto summer pastures.
To get married I did not agree at first,
You compelled me with force, to agree.

I bought a melon at the market,
I am not willing to leave my *awyl*.
My brothers remain behind,
All of them are my own flesh and blood.

Along the river grow trees,
Could I cross the river by holding on to them?
If I had been a boy when I was born,
Would I now sob as I go to another place?

Ears rise up from the barley patch,
The falcon eaglet seeks them out.[20]
When I was born and came to this earth,
God decreed that I leave my native land.

By my door flows a river,
The wind blows hard and raises its waves.
People of the *awyl* said "We will not marry you off!"
Who is the one that convinced you all?

There is a white-striped horse in the herd,
A boy standing there could not catch him.
People, be considerate toward my Dad,
Who pampered me from my childhood.

The yellow buttons bought at the market,
Why has the sewing thread snapped?
"I will not marry you off" my Dad said.
But why have you changed your mind?

Swallows are flying to the woods,
Their flapping wings touch tips of grass.
O my dear Mom who pampered me,
You are the one who pushes me, into living hell.

There are willow bushes by my door,
My sheep are left in the woods.
O *awyl*, you who spoiled me,
The people left behind are weeping.

Low apple trees are thriving,
Narrow-leaved oleaster are growing densely.
Had I been born a boy,
I would remain with you, and rightly so.

Black clouds have blotted out the sky,
My horses are tended on the grasslands.
Do not think that I am still alive,
I am the same as a corpse.

I drove my sheep to the village,
And from the village to the market.
Do not say "She did not say good-bye."
I said good-bye to all of you.

Bowls, kettles, and teapots,
Are all bought at the market.
Do not say "She did not say good-bye."
Ladies, I said farewell to you.

Golden horseshoes are made at the market,
Thousands of gold coins are their price.
Do not say "She did not say good-bye."
Brothers, I said farewell to you.

Floodwaters rush from the mountain side.
The girl's eight braids are of the same length.
Do not say "She did not say good-bye,"
Sisters-in-law, I said it to you.

I tied the dowry onto a white camel,
The loads at both sides are balanced the same.
Do not say "She did not say good-bye."
I said farewell and cried bitterly.

I bought a lock at the market,
My desire was not to get married.
To get married is to be doomed.
I wish you peace *(salam)*, my people back home!

My brownish horse stands in the herd,
I think of you with nostalgic longing.
Oh, my *awyl* is left behind,
I wish good luck to all of you.

How can I endure all the bright days?
How can I endure all the nights?
While I am at such a strange place,
Deep sorrows accompany me from daybreak till night.

The ends of rivers run into the sea,
There are animals stout and strong.
Dear Mother said "I do not marry you off."
Now you let others say "The bride is coming."

Buttons are stitched and worn at my breast.
O dear Mother, you pampered me,
You who fed me with your breast,
Of your kindness I am unworthy.

Now I wear the unlucky black clothes,
How kindhearted you are, dear Mom!
Peace be with you all your life.
May your life be long, and longer![21]

With songs such as these the wedding rites in the bride's *awyl* come to an end. The bride sings *köris* songs and thereby bids goodbye to her relatives. With the help of her brothers she mounts a horse which had been given her by her father. Her dowries are loaded on camels, and accompanied by her mother, sister-in-law, younger brothers and younger sisters, they journey to the bridegroom's *awyl*. Usually the bride dresses in red. A bride from wealthier families wears an embroidered red dress and wears a *sawkele*, that is, a Kazakh bridal coronet inlaid with precious stones and fitted with a piece of red velvet to cover her face.

Wedding Rite at the Groom's Home *(Khalyngdykh Toi)*

The father and mother of the groom sponsor a celebration to welcome the bride to their *awyl*. As the troop of people with the bride approach the bridegroom's *awyl*, the groom himself is expected to come forth to meet and welcome the bride. While the bride and her relatives wait at the point of meeting, the groom is expected to run back and notify his relatives. The sister-in-law of the bridegroom—if there is one—and other ladies then come forth to meet the bride. They lead her to her parents-in-law who are waiting in front of their yurt. While they meet, the mother-in-law distributes pieces of hard cheese, *khurt*, fried bread, *bawyrsakh*, and candies to their new daughter-in-law and to the guests. In Kazakh this is called *shashyw*, and with it the celebration has begun. Then, after her parents-in-law have entered, the bride is carried on the arms of two young ladies into the yurt. Guests who are getting on in years sit down on the seats of honor which are set up outside by the door of the yurt.

Then a lively man, charming and witty, holds the horsewhip, or a stick, or a branch to which stripes of different colors are tied, and begins the *bet ashar* or face-uncovering rite. He sings the *bet ashar* song. By way of it he introduces the bridegroom's father and mother, the elders of the *awyl*, and the clan chiefs. He also recounts the customs of the tribe.[22] While he sings he waves the horsewhip and touches the red veil that is still covering the head and face of the bride.

> I am standing here to take off your veil.
> Your mother-in-law is ready to distribute *shashyw*.
> Your father-in-law is wondering, looking at the lively scene.
> He has been waiting a very long time.
> My Dear, now you have arrived.
> From here on a new journey begins,
> The result of a new beginning.
> You found one who joins in marriage with you.
> My Dear, if you are good,
> All your relatives and friends will be happy.
> First of all, you owe greatest esteem to your father-in-law.
> He is like a big tree, green and magnificent.
> Do not consider my words to be mere casual remarks.
> One who has manners and who is well behaved,
> Is someone whom the mountain people like.
> Have you noticed your father-in-law,
> He is going to bless you!
> One who esteems her parents-in-law
> People regard as a good daughter-in-law.

Then the speaker addresses the parents-in-law:

> Now look at your child.
> Look at her carefully and do not be negligent.
> Catch that good mare from your horse-herd.
> Give it to her as a present for this first meeting.

Turning again to the bride the admonishment continues:

> Pay respect to your father-in-law!
> And if you have esteem for your mother-in-law,
> She will be like a boat floating on the river.
> Listen carefully with your ears,
> To the words and thoughts she speaks and gives.
> She will say "God bless and protect you!"
> Besides that, what else will she say?
> Do not do any unreasonable things.
> Do not cross the path in front of her.
> Do not make noises with dishes and bowls.
> Do not pour out the contents of dishes at your own will.
> Do not bang the door heavily.
> Do not lose your temper easily.
> The neighbors in your *awyl*, left and right,
> You should get along with all of them.
> These are the ways left by our ancestors.
> These are their legacy to us.

Turning toward the mother-in-law, these words are spoken:

> You, her mother-in-law, please listen to me!
> I wish to speak some words to you as well.
> Give her a present for this first meeting,
> Give her a mother camel, with a calf.

Turning again to face the bride, the speaker says:

> Pay respect to your mother-in-law!
> Your elder brother-in-law is also sitting here.
> He will get ready everything you need.
> He had a younger brother (the groom) after him.
> He will take care of all of you,
> If you are his good sister-in-law.
> When he dismounts from the horse, support him.
> Open the door for him when he enters the yurt.
> Spread the embroidered felt for him.
> When he sees you he will be glad.
> You are as beautiful as a blossom,
> All the people here will agree with me.

It would be improper not to speak such words.
You should esteem your older brother-in-law,
As you esteem your own brother.
Now you have come here from far away.
Everything is decreed by destiny.

Pay respects to your older brother-in-law!
Be on good terms with your sister-in-law,
Share your food with others.
If you are kind and gentle,
Even strangers will be on friendly terms with you.
Divide equally, and then,
Spend the money which the brothers earn.
Respect one another saying *siz* and *biz*.[23]
Do not speak to one another in gruffy voices.
I speak these words to both of you.

Older sister-in-law, are you here too?
If you get along well, you will resemble each other.
If you do get along without being jealous of one another.
If you are getting along well, you will be inseparable.
If you lose your reason, you will be harsh on each other,
You will be distant toward the other and have no dealings.
To live in harmony is the best source of income.
Do not allow good fortune to get lost.
Do not let your enemies laugh at you,
Do not let your friends become estranged from you.
Do not regard my words as nonsense.
"Where there is no unity there is no life," an old saying goes.
Give a lamb to your (new) sister-in-law!
(And you) pay respect to your older sister-in-law!
You also should esteem your younger brother-in-law.
He will respect you in return.
He will help you when you are to ride on a horse.
He will tighten the belts of your saddle.
No matter at what time you need his help,
He will be ready to help you.
Nobody detests his younger brother.
Having a younger brother is a good fortune.

You are as brother and sister, as born of one mother.
He will always be your protector.
When he returns home after work,
Get a cup ready and make some tea.
If you show concern for him,
He will show the same for you.
What I told you, please remember,
Because these are my innermost thoughts and feelings.

Pay respect to your younger brother-in-law!
You also should esteem your husband,
Remain chaste and faithful to your husband.
All my words are for the sake of your own good.
What I have in mind I have told you.
Whether you esteem your husband,
He will know whether you are good or bad.
May your love be pure and honest.
Both of you must trust each other.
Keep these words in your mind,
Which were spoken by the elders.
You should also listen to my words,
Accept the blessings given by the elders.
And among what is good and what is bad,
Distinguish carefully.
Set a fine example all around.
Be polite to everyone.
Care for your parents-in-law who are old,
Look after them as if they were children.
Make their beds soft.
Cover them with quilts that they do not catch cold.
Keep your room clean and everything in order.
Do not sleep in late in the morning.
Get up early and make a fire.
Do all the work you can do.
Prove worthy of your parents' love.
Prove worthy of their hopes.
Many people have gathered here today,
They asked me to take off your veil.
And our customary saying goes:

"I will take away the red veil from your face;
Pay your respects to everyone."
Pay respect and bend your knees.
These are the old customs of the Kazakhs.
Pour oil into the fire and pray.[24]

Notes

1. Clan membership is obtained through the father, and the chief's name tends to become the name of the clan. Some ambiguity exists in nomenclature. While, as a general rule, members of the same clan *(ruw)* cannot marry one another, the situation becomes ambiguous in the case of larger tribes *(ruw)* that consist of a number of smaller clans (which are also called *ruw*). Thus, members of the large Naiman group frequently intermarry, while members within its component clans cannot.

2. The word *öltiri* is formed from *öl* (dead) and *tiri* (alive). Gifts aside from livestock, which are given at this ceremonial occasion *(toi)* by the groom's side to the family of the bride, include also pieces of fabric. White cloth is included in honor of the deceased ancestors of the girl's family.

3. The traditional meaning was that the bridegroom goes to the bride's awyl secretly and quietly. When marriages were still arranged by elders, this could have been the first occasion at which he was able to see his bride. Nowadays the groom may openly visit his bride before the wedding. This is why the Go Quiet Ritual *(uryn baryw toi)* has now changed as well. Brothers and sisters-in-law of the bride will invite some young people to their *awyl*, prepare food, and amuse themselves together with the groom.

4. "Kök" means gray, and "par" is derived from "böri" (wolf); "kökpar tartew" means gray wolf grabbing.

5. For the sake of civility and education, this interpretation of the game ought to be insisted on, perhaps, as the official version. There is, nevertheless, a more direct explanation concerning the wolf epithet on this fierce game of horsemanship. Any outside visitor inevitably is stunned by the ferociousness of this sport. It seems therefore also plausible that from the outset the Central Asiatic riders were "playing wolf" with their victim which then, naturally, would be a domestic animal.

6. Perhaps it should be noted, here, that poetry and song contests are equally cherished by Kazakh young people. Their singing contests *(akhyn aitys)*—see Chapter 3—serve as gentler alternatives to heroic games and the thrills of horsemanship.

7. Collected by Li Zengxiang during winter of 1956, in Shäweshek county, of the Tarbaghatai Prefecture. Sung by Khuwnanbai Khozhanai-uly.

8. The gold buttons symbolize her sister-in-law, who will be very close to her in her new home.

9. Sapymülik and Zhamal, as well as Zylyigha and Jüsip, are married couples who appear in many Kazakh tales.

10. From *Shalghyn*, 1980, 2, pp. 72-74.

11. This Kazakh proverb ranks romantic love above pragmatic considerations. When a girl has found her beloved, her parents should not require betrothal gifts from the bridegroom. Of course, this is wishful opinion expressed by single young men.

12. This refers to an unidentified incident over which the mother at one time may or may not have scolded her daughter—a trivial omission.

13. From *Shalghyn*, 1980, 2, pp. 74-75.

14. Collected by Li Zengxiang during winter 1956, in Shaghantoghai county, Tarbaghatai prefecture. Sung by Sembai Ämirkhan-uly.

15. Collected by Li Zengxiang during winter 1956, in Shäweshek county, Tarbaghatai prefecture. Sung by Khuwnanbai Khozhanai-uly.

16. *Syngsyma* songs are songs of mourning and lament. The verb *syngsy* means to weep or to cry.

17. From *Shughyla* 1980, 2, pp. 75f.

18. *Ibid.*, pp. 77f.

19. From *Shalghyn*, 1980, 1, pp. 77f.

20. As far as we know, nowhere in the world do eaglets eat the grain of barley, but in this Kazakh bridal song of sorrow they seem to do just that.

21. From *Mura (Legacy)*, 1988, 1, pp. 63-68.

22. Kazakh tribes vary some of these customs. For example, the attire of women in the Kerei tribe, in the Tarbaghatai and Altai prefecture, differs from that of women in the Khyzai, Alban, and Suwan tribes who live in the Ile prefecture; scarfs are worn differently. Or, the choice of words in everyday speech may need to be adjusted. For instance, if an elder's name in the tribe or clan happens to be Khairakhbai, then a grindstone (*khairakh* in Kazakh), must be referred to with another name.

23. *Siz* and *biz* is the polite form of "you" and "we." *Siz* is the personal pronoun to address persons who are older. The polite form *biz* (we, our) is used to substitute for "me" and "my" when one is speaking to an older person. For example, *mening awlymda* (in my *awyl*) becomes *bizding awlymyzda* (in our awyl).

24. From *Mura* 1, 1988, pp. 69-71. As far as fire is concerned, it is divine. Fire purifies and drives away evil spirits; fire protects the family. With this religious gesture the bride becomes a member of the groom's family who pray in a similar manner.

Chapter 6

Marriage in the Epics

From Kazakh epics, especially from romantic epics, one can learn much about traditional marriage customs, about pledges and promises, about honor and dishonor, about relationships and interactions among families and clans, about labor and livelihood, and even a few things about funeral customs.

Kazakh epics feature their own distinct style and rhythm.[1] They are treasure troves of historical data and allude to many societal and nationwide connections. Some of the larger Kazakh epic poems have lines which are counted by the tens of thousands. These epics have been acclaimed as the essence of Kazakh history, as gems of Kazakh folk literature, as monuments to heroes, and as mirrors for Kazakh national consciousness. Heroic epics synthesize all the aggressive optimism and the positive Kazakh outlook on life; they brand the confederation of Kazakh peoples with its unique stamp of nationality.

129

Famous Kazakh epics are "Alpamis" (from the 10th and 11th Century C.E.), "Khoblandy" (10th to 12th Century), "Hero Targhyn" (14th and 15th Century), "Khambar" (16th Century), "Hero Esimbek" (17th Century), "Hero Khabanbai" (18th Century), and "Arkhalykh" (19th Century).

Alongside these epics of heroism, love poems of epic proportions also occupy an important place in the repertoire of Kazakh folk literature. These poetic works sing the praises of marital love, and they dwell with beautiful words on the struggles that lovers must overcome in a world were the bloodshed of heroes tend to over-shadow them.

One of the most famous love epics is "Khozy Körpesh and Bajan Sulyw" (9th and 10th Century), named after two young lovers. Then there is "The Girl Zhibek" (18th Century) which, together with "Salyiha and Saman," remains among the most beloved stories among the Kazakhs of Xinjiang.[2]

Kazakh epics tell of a variety of customs by which marriages were arranged. In this chapter we explain three traditional ways for which ample evidence can found. They are *khalyngmal*, *bel khuda*, and *ämen'ger*.

The Practice of Khalyngmal

The very ancient and lengthy epics of the Kazakh people fore-mostly rhapsodize about heroism and strength, but occasionally they also dwell on love and its fulfillment in marriage. The ancient bedrock of Kazakh marriage customs is *khalyngmal*. It is tradition that regulates inheritance and that, more than anything else in Kazakh history and society, has determined the subordinate status of women to men, and the subordination of both partners to family, clan, and tribe.

The word *khalyngmal* in Kazakh language consists of two parts. The ancient Turkic root of *khalyng* means "numerous" and *mal* means "livestock." Other scholars trace the *khalyng* in *khalyngmal* to *khalyng-dykh* which means "fiancee." The historical connection between these two root meanings is quite obvious. Considering both of these linguistic possibilities together, we can observe how all along in actual practice the tradition of *khalyngmal* pertained to engagement, to an agreement of betrothal, as well as to payments in the form of livestock. Betrothal gifts in nomadic Kazakh society have traditionally consisted mostly of livestock. The animals are given by the bridegroom to the bride's family.

The livelihood of the Kazakh people is still today based primarily upon raising livestock. Their handicraft industries have not yet become separated from practicing animal husbandry, and an industrial economy has not yet been added. The exchange of commodities is by and large still accomplished by barter, and livestock is their currency of exchange. Thus, in accordance with their means of production, not only the exchange of goods but also exchanges of human labor and of people, such as wives, are still very much linked with the business of raising livestock. The nomadic way of herding determines the lives of the rich as well as of the poor.

Of course, there is also an Islamic moral dimension attached to *khalyngmal* livestock payments. Goods paid to the family of a bride might as well be seen as a kind of guarantee for good treatment of the wife by her husband and his family.

Four kinds of animals have traditionally been used for *khalyngmal* payments—camels, horses, cows, and sheep. Along with these are paid fabrics, clothing, and nowadays also money. The amount of payment depends on one's social position and on the amount of property that is being owned by both parties in a marriage agreement.

The general result of this practice is not difficult to guess, and the Kazakh saying summarizes it well: "The rich marry the rich, and they receive fine horses. The poor marry the poor, and they receive only bundles." Thus, among poorer Kazakhs a *khalyngmal* payment may amount to five or six mature animals, while among the rich the number of animals can run into the hundreds. In ancient times when a Kazakh girl was married off, and depending on the amount of *khalyngmal* paid by the bridegroom, the girl often brought along her own dowry, which could include livestock as well—even male and female slaves.

Because payment of *khalyngmal* has become a precondition for marriage, poor herdsmen often were unable to marry in accordance with this system. Another practice therefore evolved alongside *khalyngmal*. Poor people married in accordance with *kharsy khudalykh*. This means that two families exchanged their daughters to become daughters-in-law in each other's families. In this manner, both families remitted *khalyngmal* by way of canceling out each other's indebtedness, in an even trade. Payment and acceptance of *khalyngmal*, in any case, meant that the marriages were arranged by parents and elders.

According to the custom of *khalyngmal* a man was able to marry several wives. Ordinarily this meant that the amount paid for each wife was different. Each successive marriage required more than the preceding one. The rationale often given for this difference is the increasing disparity in the ages of the groom and the bride. Of course a very wealthy man who had his mind set on marrying a certain beautiful young girl would not easily shirk from a sizeable payment. Given all these time-honored adaptations to a nomadic herder economy, and given these religiously sanctioned ways for balancing property and power, it can easily be understood how Kazakh womankind has become subservient, or remained in that state.

Bel Khuda in "Khozy Körpesh and Bajan Sulyw"

Ancient Kazakh conditions and customs can nowadays best be reconstructed by contemplating the old national epics. Among many nomadic societies in Asia, epics in general have to this day remained living traditions. They still provide ancestral paradigms and heroic models for present-day living. They have come to function in Kazakh life, still today, as a second rank of sacred writings—which is secondary only to the Qur'an.

Khozy Körpesh and Bajan Sulyw are a boy and a girl, primary characters in a long epic poem of 2600 lines. The poem bears their names as its title. This particular epic comes from the 9th or 10th Century and ranks among the longest and oldest in the Kazakh repertoire. Scholars have begun to collect versions of that tradition as early as 1834. Its first edition was printed in Kazan, in 1878. Subsequently it has been translated into Russian by G. N. Tvertin and into German by Wilhelm Radloff.[3] During the 1940s and 1950s, Kazakh writers in the former Soviet Union arranged this epic for drama and have made it into a movie.

"Khozy Körpesh and Bajan Sulyw" has been handed down as well among the million or so Kazakhs who live in China. While the Russian and the Chinese version are very similar, they differ enough to warrant a fresh translation of excerpts from the latter. The two versions differ primarily in their conclusions. While the Russian version ends as a tragedy, the Chinese counterpart resolves into comedy. For the specific purpose of explaining the Kazakh practice of *bel khuda* we have selected several relevant portions of the Chinese version for translation into English.[4]

The story's primary characters are Kharabai, father of the girl Bajan Sulyw, and Sarybai, the father of the boy Khozy Körpesh. Both fathers are men of wealth *(bai)*. They met each other by chance during a long hunting expedition, and in this manner they became acquainted with one another:

"I am a headsman of ten thousand,
But I am worthless.
I am already eighty-three with no-one to rely on.
My name is 'Kharabai' and I am hopeless."

"O my Dear One *(Khareke)*! I did not know you.
To Allah's arrangement I am obedient.
I am already seventy-five with no-one to rely on.
I too am a loner, my name is Sarybai."

"Oh, you too suffer hardship without children.
When you get a child, you will be satisfied.
I am already eighty-three, I am really without hope,
Whereas you still can hope for what may lie ahead."

"O my Dear One, both of us are now acquainted.
It is God who led us to meet each other.
I notice you are older than I by eight years.
Eighty-three and seventy-five are nearly the same."
. . . .

Allah bestowed on them much wealth,
From their mouths they vowed to each other,
Two men, standing on land inhabited by no-one,
In God's name became friends for this world and the next.

"We heed Allah's arrangement,
And because we are esteemed men in the people's eyes.
If by chance we get a son or girl,
Without betrothal gifts let them be married."

Sometime after their agreement Sarybai went on a hunting expedition with Kharabai. He suddenly fell ill, and his words to Kharabai were these:

"Maybe you cannot meet me anymore.
Can our promises be kept or not?
We swore to be relatives by marriage.
If you get a girl, will you give her to me or not?"

"To people who dislike me, I am a stream drying up.
To people who love me, I am a fountainhead.
Please do not worry. I will not break my promise.
If that day comes, I will give my girl to your son."

Sarybai's corpse was left in the wilds. Kharabai carried off his bags and returned homeward. On his way he met some of his own people, and some of Sarybai's people, who came to announce good news to the two chiefs in the wilds:

Dear One! *(Khareke!)* We meet you here in the wilds.
All of us are men of Sarybai,
Madame Sarybai has given birth to a son.
We are here in the wilds to bring greetings to him.
. . . .

O Dear Brother, we found you here in the wilds.
You will see how beautiful the infant is.
Dear Brother, our sister-in-law has born a child.
Now we shall see what *süyinshi* you will give us."[5]

Thus, along his way, Kharabai learned that Sarabai's wife has born a son. Upon returning home he discovered that his own wife had given birth to a girl. He filled ninety skins with *khymyz*—fermented mare's milk—and together with his people he went to Sarabai's yurt to ascertain what actually has happened.

Sarabai's riches were as wide as the grassland.
In the cradle on the bedding lay Khozy, like the moon.

When the stupid old man saw him,
He fled away as if he had seen a devil.
. . . .

On his way back he stopped at a place.
And that stupid old man then ordered,
To slice the ninety bags of *khymyz*,
To let it flow away like a stream of water.

The visit of Kharabai at Sarybai's yurt has brought to the attention
of the people the fact, that Kharabai and Sarybai had made a *bel khuda*
agreement between their two families. A few years passed, and
Sarybai's wife send a messenger to Kharabai's home to make inquiries
about the pending engagement. Kharabai then retorted:

"Shut your mouth! I will not listen to any of your words.
I do not recognize such words as ever having been said.
Tuck your tail between your legs and get away.
I will not marry my girl to an orphan."

In order to better shirk his obligation toward the Sarybai family,
Kharabai began moving away as far as possible from the other's *awyl*.
During the move Kharabai's livestock was seriously threatened by a
drought. Khodar, a Mongol hero of the Torghawyt tribe, offered to
help Kharabai and to dig a well, on condition that he could marry Bajan
Sulyw. Kharabai agreed with Khodar's condition and thereby saved his
livestock.

But Bajan Sulyw did not agree. She knew that there was a fiancee
by a *bel khuda* agreement, and she wanted to marry Khozy Körpesh.
The boy Khozy Körpesh, on the other hand, also knew about the
agreement, and he longed for Bajan Sulyw.

One day Khozy Körpesh said goodbye to his mother, to his
relatives and his homeland. After climbing across mountain after
mountain, and after journeying over hill and dale, he came to the
homestead where Kharabai lived. To make contact with Bajan Sulyw
he disguised himself as a shepherd. At daytime he herded sheep and at
nighttime he performed household duties for Kharabai. It was not long
before he could contact Bajan Sulyw.

A shepherd boy came and revealed his true face,
The girl Bajan was cheerful and afraid.
As they came to know each other
They embraced warmly and happily.

No-one knows how long they did embrace.
Two (adopted) girls stood next to them and shed tears of joy.
The two girls were like the sun and the moon.
They led the couple to a yurt near the settlement.

The shepherd boy wanted to marry his sweetheart,
And keep his mind on guard against his enemy.
As shepherd he dressed at daytime, as Khozy during night.
He stayed with this family a year long.

When Khodar noticed that Khozy was the sweetheart of Bajan
Sulyw, he treated him high handedly. This aroused Khozy to great
indignation, and he resolved to teach Khodar a lesson:

Khozy with his arrows shot down flying birds,
Game animals absent, he shot at floating targets in the river.
Many stakes (*zheli*) were by the coral,
With his thumb he pushed them into the earth.

The people were amazed at Khozy's strength.
He rode after horses to show his prowess.
When he grasped the tails of these horses,
Those fiery steeds got tied up, submissively.
. . . .

Khozy then rode over to Khodar,
He caught hold of Khodar's back.
And even though Khodar tried to escape,
He fell from his horse's back.
. . . .

Khozy showed another skill.
He picked up Khodar and clutched him under his thigh.[6]
He rode to a deep stagnant water puddle,

Dropped Khodar into it, and rode off slowly.
. . . .

They set ten hoes in a row, stood up as a target.
Brave young men gathered for fun.
Khozy rose and said *Bismillä!* (In the name of Allah!)
And his arrow flew through ten hoes in a row.
. . . .

Khozy again went to Khodar for wrestling.
Does Khodar know what is honor and shame?
Khozy put Khodar at the bottom,
Another ninety of his partners upon him as ballast.

"Hey Tazsha,"[7] said Khodar, "when did I offend you?
You treat me like this. You bully me.
I drank too much *khymyz* in my yurt;
That is why my pants are wet with shit and urine."

The relationship which existed between Khozy and Bajan became
known to other people, and to Khodar:

Khodar obtained confidential information from others.
His heart burned with the fire of envy.
His angry buttocks broke the saddle.
He bit off a piece of flesh from his own thumb.

He dared not to go and confront Khozy,
Instead he turned back to Kharabai's yurt:
"Kharabai khan, your girl was taken by your enemy.
You have to pay me for digging the well."

"You are one of the most sensible in your clan.
I will call forty young ladies and girls.
Let them invite Khozy to come here.
Let him drink some wine with poison.

If you fight him you will fail.
Overly anxious for quick results you will lose everything.

With an ingenious scheme we can kill him.
No-one will want to fight you, and my girl belongs to you."
. . . .

A girl led a horse to Khozy,
He mounted the brown one and rode away.
Wine and poison was vomited from his mouth.
The mane of the brown horse fell off (from the potion).

After Khozy had again come to himself he turned back to Kharabai's *awyl*. He began to fight:

Khozy was the strongest in those days.
When Khodar saw him, he dared not to flee.
"You bully small folk, you went too far!"
Khozy aimed at his breast and shot him.

Hero Khozy returned to his men.
But before doing so he killed him and cut off his head.
Returning to his people, shouting and cheering,
He hung it behind his saddle, a thong through the lips.

With the despicable Kharabai, his prospective father-in-law, Khozy proceeded in similar fashion:

No-one dared to lift his head and look.
With his sword Khozy slashed the whole body.
He hung the corpse on a tree for everyone to see.
He cut Kharabai into pieces and threw him to the dogs.

From these epic excerpts one can see that Khozy and Bajan initially did not know each other. Yet, at some point their affections were aroused for each other. They were enabled to surmount all kinds of difficulties to win mutual happiness. Their love and their strength to endure were triggered by the knowledge of a *bel khuda* agreement concerning them. The prominent character in this long epic, Kharabai, is a dud because he disregarded *bel khuda*. Moreover Khodar, a Mongolian spoiler of the Kazakh order, had come from the outside. Thus, estimating on the basis of this epic, one may conclude that in ancient days the Kazakh *bel khuda* covenants were deemed sacred. They were part and parcel of the ancient Kazakh marriage law.

Ämen'ger in "Khyz Zhibek."

Ämen'ger, too, is a Kazakh marriage tradition.[8] Its practice harmonizes nicely with similar customs in Semitic lands. The question of whether it had been a Kazakh practice in pre-Islamic times, or whether it was brought by way of Islam, is historically significant but must for the time being be left unanswered. The history of Islam itself is rooted in the nomadic and pastoral cultures of the Near East. Turkic herders of Central Asia became naturally attracted to the religion of Islam because it resonated well with kindred pastoralist traditions beyond Arabia. It also provided justification and encouragement for dealing with neighboring kingdoms and empires. The religion of Islam in the Near East was affected not only by its ancient nomadic roots, but also by the way it learned to define itself, with protestant fervor, in relation to the advanced Byzantine and Persian empires.

"Khyz Zhibek" is a popular Kazakh romantic epic. Its title contains the name of its heroine that translates into English as "Silk Girl." *Khyz* means girl, *zhibek* means silk, and both words together add up to a Kazakh girl's name. This epic of approximately seven thousand lines was composed, perhaps, during the 17th Century, and it is one of the most artistically wrought love epics known. During the 1880s Russian scholars have recorded the gist of the story in prose, and since 1900 it has been published several times in Kazakh. During the 1950s some writers in Russia arranged it for drama and also made it into a movie.

"Khyz Zhibek" was handed down at the Chinese side of the border as well. Here, it is a much longer poem than in Russia, and its plot has become extremely complicated, full of conflicts and contradictions. The scenes of struggle are almost endless, and that fact has not escaped some scholars of Kazakh literature abroad.[9]

A rich man *(bai)* appears in this epic. His name is Bazarbai. He is the khan of his tribe. He had nine sons of whom all have died. In the hope of getting another child he married six wives. While he was already at the advanced age of eighty, his last married wife bore him a son who was named Tölegen. After nine years she bore him another

son who was given the name of Sansyzbai. When seventeen years old
Tölegen could not find a bride in his region, he therefore started on a
long journey in search of one, far away.

> Saddle and gear decorated with precious stones,
> He leads more than a hundred companions.
> Nine dromedary camels carry silver and gold.
> Another five youths are assigned to be his servants.
> May God bless these warriors!
> Forty camels are carrying tea and sugar.
> Everything they need is carried along.
> So, with relatives he goes forth, during Nawryz.[10]

> Two hundred and fifty horses,
> Selected from the horse herd.
> How many days do they expend along their way?
> Not very few, along that very long way.
> At last they reached the river Ak Zhajykh.

A rich man, a khan, lives there. His name is Syrlybai. He has six
sons and a daughter. The daughter's name is Khyz Zhibek. While these
people are moving about, from one place to another, Tölegen follows
them on horseback:

> The gray horse strides with a majestic gait,
> Light radiates from its eyes.
> The breast straps are decorated with gold,
> Dangling at its chest.
> While it is stepping on black earth,
> The earth is trembling like a willow bridge.
> Its four legs remain steady,
> While its hooves are touching its girth.
> While it is galloping on stones,
> The stones are making noises of clatter.
> Dust is being kicked up like a whirlwind,
> The muscles of its hind legs are vibrating.
> Sparks fly from its four hooves,
> Like steel and flint knocking together.
> Listening to the sounds he makes,

Like gurgling water running down a mountain.
Sweat runs down his back,
He wets the stirrup belts while galloping.
Steady—a bowl of water on its back would not spill,
How nicely it canters along in that steady pace!
Even with the reins pulled back,
It rivals in speed a flying bird.
And reins pulled back, it arrives,
Tölegen's two hands have pins and needles.

When they strike camp and move to another site, Kazakh nomads load all their belongings on camels. The people ride on horses, men and women alike. But because Zhibek is afraid of dust, she never rides on a horse. Ordinarily she sits on a cart with a cover.

A cart, hitched up to three black horses,
Those three, galloping like running water.
Their manes and tails decorated with owl feathers,
To their foreheads are tied strips of red cloth.
The wooden parts of her cart,
They are painted in a variety of colors.
Silks and satins, red and green,
Comprise the cover on her carriage.
On the covering patterns are embroidered,
Decorated with precious stones.
Of the beauty of her wagon,
There is no likeness in this world.
. . . .

Three girls are sitting next to her,
Wearing hats of otter skin.
Today Zhibek looks like the full moon,
She is only fourteen years old.
Her mouth is small, eyes are full of tenderness,
Everyone falls in love with her at first sight.
When Tölegen first sees Zhibek
He feels as if he lost his wits.
Her two eyes are full of light,
Just as bright water running from a fountain.

Her thirty teeth are like pearls,
A red tongue is surrounded by them.
On her spotless white forehead,
Her eyebrows stretch like crescent moons.
And furthermore, like willow boughs,
Her eyelashes are long and thick.
Her face is in ruddy health.
Those two heavy golden earrings,
Her ears can hardly sustain them.
Her braids are swaying in the breeze,
Her neck looks like a bronze tea pot.
Her skin is smooth as white silk,
Fragrance exudes from her.
The beauty of Khyz Zhibek
Is like the white snow of March.
The red color on her white face
Is like blood of a white hen spilled on fresh snow.
The looks of her two cheeks
Is like the brightness of summer days.
Her voice is clear and melodious,
Sounding like the water of Zamzam fountain.[11]
Her arms are round and soft,
Like the handle of a white hammer.
Two apples are bulging at her breast,
Like the muscles of a male camel's thighs.
And even though not everyone could marry her,
Once you have seen her, you would feel satisfied,
As if you reached your goal.
Even if Zhibek were to expire,
People who find her remains
Would still approach to kiss her face.

Quite understandably, Tölegen falls in love at first sight with this wonderful girl. He sends someone to act as a go-between and matchmaker. He wants to give *öltiri toi,* the portion of *khalyngmal* gifts that is given during the first round of engagement.[12]

Tölegen is overjoyed,
He it to be married to Zhibek.

Servants are preparing the *öltiri*,
Are rounding up the animals needed.
They prepare two hundred fifty horses,
They load shoe-shaped silver ingots.
They approach nearer and nearer,
To the *awyl* of Syrlybai.

. . . .

That being completed they talk about the wedding,
A special wedding yurt is readied.
Relatives and guests are invited for days,
Khan Syrlybai holds the *öltiri* ceremony.
The nights of June are too short,
Why does the day break so quickly?
The day-times of summer are much too long,
They last too long til sunset when the sun tarries to set.
The newly-weds have been together for three months,
Now the time has come for the return.

Tölegen prepares to return to his own *awyl*. Because there have
been many young chieftain's sons who have sent intermediaries to
Zhibek's father, whom Zhibek rejected, she is afraid that someone
might want to kill Tölegen on his way home. Tölegen answers Zhibek:

"My dear Zhibek, what are you worrying about?
I have a younger brother, Sansyzbai.
And if the worst should happen,
Sansyzbai will lead his men and come to your tribe."

This does not only mean that Sansyzbai will come and help her. It also
implies that if some misfortune should befall the groom, Sansyzbai
would inherit his brother's wife in accordance with Kazakh custom.

After Tölegen returns to his home he does not tell his parents what
happened. He is afraid they would oppose his course of action. After
some time, nevertheless, Tölegen asks his father to give him permission
to go and meet his bride again. His father refuses to give his consent.
But because Tölegen has promised Zhibek to come back next summer,
he insists on going. Before he sets out on his journey he tells his
younger brother:

"Let me tell you the truth,
But promise me not to tell others.
You are my brother, my dear one,
Fighting with enemies you are my helper.
As if my words were of two kinds,
Why should I not live up to what I vowed!
Your beautiful sister-in-law is Khyz Zhibek,
I am going to get her.
For the sake of Khyz Zhibek,
I am going there to see her.
On my way there are dangers.
If something happens, this or that,
Then your sister-in-law, as valuable as silk,
You yourself go and find.
If something happens, this or that,
Then your sister-in-law, as valuable as silk,
Take her then and love her."

. . . .

Along the road Tölegen is killed by enemies who are led by Bekejan.

Seven years pass. Zhibek still refuses to get married to another person and devotes herself wholeheartedly to the burden of waiting for Tölegen. At last Bekejan tells her the truth about Tölegen's death in the context of an antiphonal song. News spreads to Zhibek's brothers, and her six brothers kill Bekejan.

All the while, Tölegen's parents still do not know anything about their son's death. On that account the old couple suffers very much until, at last, they are confined to their beds. They are unable to recover. During this time Sansyzbai grows up to be seventeen. With the permission of his parents he starts on a journey to find his brother, Tölegen.

The clan of Syrlybai has meanwhile been conquered by Horen, a khan among the Kalmuks. Horen arbitrarily gives orders to prepare for his marriage with Zhibek, but Syrlybai refuses.

Syrlybai speaks with determination:
"No-one can destroy Muslims.
Please deliver my message to Horen, the khan.

Do not let him set his mind on my girl!
She is someone's widow already,
Let him not mention his thought to her.
The girl of a Muslim,
She is not going to be brought to hell (*tozakh*).
If we betray our religion,
All of us will be punished."

. . . .

When Khan Horen hears all this,
He rolls up his sleeves (and resolves)
"If he does not give me his girl,
I will butcher his whole clan."

. . . .

When Zhibek learns about this, she cries,
And her tears flow like a fountain:
"To a foreigner like a Kalmuk?
How can my heart be content?
I have no alternative but to yield.
What else can I say to my people
About the sufferings which they would endure?
Let me suffer instead.
When I step across the Kalmuk's threshold,
At that very moment I will die.
Celebrate the ceremony for forty days,
Conduct games for thirty days.
Invite children of six years and older,
Do also not forget old men of sixty and over.
On that day, call them to the ceremony,
And let my heavy heart be comforted by this."

According to Zhibek's suggestion, the Kalmuks hold a grandiose ceremony. But just when the ceremony begins, Sansyzbai arrives with his men. Through a variety of channels they learn that Tölegen, Sansyzbai's brother, had been killed and that the Kalmuks are now forcing Zhibek to marry Horen. Sansyzbai secretly contacts Zhibek who, at first, cannot believe that all this is true. At their first meeting they plot their escape.

Zhibek turns her head and looks,
Is looking with fixed eyes.
(It seems) as if Tölegen's skin had been flayed
And is worn over his brother's body.
"This is the one of eight years ago,
This is Tölegen," she thinks.

. . . .

"While I have not seen you, my heart was still lost,
When I saw you I recalled his last words.
When I saw you, O Sister-in-law,
How cheerful my heart became.
We must not remain long. We must return.
Please tell me your decision."

When she heard these words she recoiled:
"Let me ask you a riddle.
A sister-in-law is inherited by the younger brother,
People said it so long ago.
What is the answer to this riddle?"

. . . .

"I will be there tomorrow noon,
Wait for me at Kharaghash.
My Light *(Shyraghym)*, Sansyzbai,
Where you take me, decide for yourself.
I am a bird that belongs to you.
I have waited eight years for this.
No other wish do I have."

Zhibek steals Horen's horse and sword and escapes with Sansyzbai. When Horen discovers that he has been cheated by Zhibek he
summons his men. He holds Kharshygha, Syrlybai's right hand man,
as a hostage to lead the way while tracking Sansyzbai.

But Horen's men cannot keep up with him. They fall behind, and
Horen pursues alone. After eleven days he catches up with them.
Sansyzbai and Horen agree to a three-stage duel. Already during the
first round Horen is killed:

He uses his strength, he shoots an arrow,
He thinks that Sansyzbai will be dead.
A suit of armor with nine sheets,
Not even one sheet does the arrow pierce.
He feels amazed and he regrets.
One sees it on that Kalmuk's face.
. . . .
Now it is Sansyzbai's turn,
And he counts his arrows.
First he puts on a cast iron arrow.
The force with which he draws is proper.
He aims right at his heart.
He draws the bow carefully.
. . . .

The arrow whizzes and pierces
His thick breast, thick as a door.
The arrow pierces through and flies beyond.
Flies on at yonder side, far away.
. . . .

The arrow flies beyond,
At last it reaches a mountain slope.
It neither tumbles nor falls sideways,
There it still raises a cloud of dust.
. . . .

Horen drops from his horse,
If he had not dropped, how could he have endured?
This pig iron arrow, shot through his breast,
Came out at the other side.
Because of the crimes of the Kalmuks,
Horen was thus brought to hell (*tozakh*).

Having defeated his opponent, Sansyzbai comes to Zhibek, cheerfully. And from his heart he speaks:

"Wait Zhibek! Wait!
Am I warm in your heart?" he asks.

"Horen was killed by lightning.
There is nothing to be anxious about.
Now I belong to you alone.
Am I not in your heart?" he asks.
"Now you are in my heart.
Do you understand what I mean?" he says.
Zhibek smiles faintly,
She knows and understands what he means.
Even though she has difficulty expressing it,
Her heart smiles with joy.

. . . .

Kharshygha, meanwhile, has led the men of Horen into the desert, to bury them there in a sandstorm. Then he, together with one of Zhibek's brothers, and with another ten men, track Sansyzbai to learn who killed Horen and how Zhibek is faring:

Sansyzbai and Zhibek return to his parents,
Khyz Zhibek gets off her horse.
She leads her horse and comes nearer.[13]
Tölegen's mother is standing,
Crying before them, over there.
An old man, Bazarbai, arises.
He also wants to come and welcome them.
From every place to which horses can trot,
From those places people come to them.
They read the Qur'an and recite blessings,
For Tölegen they give offerings (to God).
Wounds in their hearts are healed,
Happiness and joy replace their grief and sorrow.
From the day of this beginning,
A forty days ceremony is celebrated.
They decorate a white yurt,
They set it up especially for Zhibek.

Kharshygha and the others also arrive at Bazarbai's *awyl*. When Zhibek sees that her brother is with them, she is happy and grateful.

They slaughter a white sheep with a yellow head,
While many guests are gathering.[14]
"From the beginning my heart was joined (with Tölegen),
No-one else could attract my love.
'One who bites you, keep away from him,
And one who invites you, go with him,' as our saying goes.
I was tethered from the beginning.
I cannot give my heart to anyone else."
. . . .

As God has joined us together,
I am longing for his face, wholeheartedly.
I must not betray
The rules of our ancestors.
. . . .

Bazarbai's *awyl* holds a grand ceremony to welcome guests and
relatives who come to the feast. They celebrate Zhibek's and Sansyzbai's wedding.

One celebration after another,
Many yellow-headed sheep are slaughtered.
From the Zhalbaghaily clan (of Bazarbai's tribe),
Khans and common people have gathered.
Stint not property nor livestock,
Guests are entertained sumptuously and royally.
The wedding ceremony is celebrated forty days,
Games and sports are held for thirty days.
All kinds of celebrations,
One more extravagant than the preceding one.
Zhibek is covered with a *zhelek,*
Many owl feathers are attached to her head,
A tradition which came from ancient times.[15]
Duwgha (prayers) are read by the elders.
. . . .

The wedding and the rites
Are celebrated without a snag.
The guests have returned home.

It is the time, precisely,
Which Sansyzbai has promised Zhibek,
That together they go to visit her parents.
The next year that same time,
Old Bazarbai was happy.
With newly regained vigor,
He deeply bowed to everyone.
Saying "Thank you!" sincerely,
Two hundred horses are driven to his relative.
Another thirty camels are hitched together,
Gold, silver, sugar and tea.
Carpets, rugs, silks and satins,
All these carried on ten camels.
And all these goods are placed before them (the inlaws).
They may take what they like.
Many greetings are spoken to his new relatives,
And many thanks are still to be said.
Having assembled the people of his clan,
To pay respect to their new relatives,
They accompany their guests a great distance,
Together, to see them off.

As a window to Kazakh culture, the romantic epic "Khyz Zhibek" opens up a wide range of Kazakh wedding traditions and displays a wealth of ethnological information. Its primary ethos establishes the *ämen'ger* principle as an important ingredient among Kazakh marriage traditions. The multiple authors of this epic, over time, have come from a broad spectrum of old Kazakh society. And it is significant that they have focused first on the affection between Tölegen and his younger brother Sansyzbai. Tölegen risked taking his second journey because he had a younger brother. He instructed that younger brother: "If something happens... you go and meet... and love your sister-in-law."

Before she consented, Zhibek inquired several times about Tölegen's relatives. She knew that her marriage with him has some assurance for the future because he had a brother. Zhibek's father, Syrlybai, also agreed to her marriage because he knew that Tölegen had a younger brother. Thus, when Sansyzbai in due time went to search after his vanished brother he, in fact, went to bring home his sister-in-law.

In "Khyz Zhibek" all the honorable characters subscribe to the *ämen'ger* rule. They do so with the same intensity as earlier in the "Khozy Köpesh and Bajan Sulyw" epic the *bel khuda* principle was espoused. Thus endorsed, and popularly sustained by old epic poetry, *khalyngmal, bel khuda*, and *ämen'ger* have become sacred principles in traditional Kazakh common law. The latter of these three, no doubt, has received an extra impulse of support from the religion of Islam.

Notes

1. Most epics have meters of seven syllables per line, occasionally also eight or ten. Ordinary songs feature eleven syllables per line, and occasionally seven or eight. When epics are sung, their tunes adjust to the content and, occasionally, they are interrupted with spoken portions.
2. The names of Salyiha and Saman are frequently mentioned in Kazakh conversation. These two ideal lovers eloped secretly and fled together. Salyiha was recaptured by her father's men and Saman was left wounded in the mountains. By the time Saman finally approached her homestead again, to liberate her, she had committed suicide from grief. Saman died as well.
3. A translation by G. N. Tvertin, into Russian rhyme, appeared in 1927 and 1935. Wilhelm Radloff (1837–1918) published a German translation in *Proben der Volksliteratur der türkischen Stämme (10 vols.)*, vol. 3. St. Petersburg, 1870.
4. Translated from "Khozy Körpesh and Bajan Sulyw," in *Shalghyn*, 4: 34-75. Urumqi: People's Publishing House of Xinjiang, 1980. *Bel khuda* refers to a prenatal marriage agreement which becomes effective if the children, betrothed in the womb, are of opposite sex. *Bel* here means "belly" and refers to pregnancy and womb. *Khuda* means "relatives by marriage."
5. *Süyinshi* are gifts given to a messenger who brings good tidings.
6. He tucked him under after the manner in which it is done in *lakh tartyw*, a riders' game played for the possession of a headless goat.
7. *Tazsha* literally means "little baldhead." In this instance it is used as a contemptuous name and insult for a shepherd boy.
8. The meaning of *ämen'ger* may be derived from old Turkic words. The root *äm* may be derived from *ab* (family, house), *-eng* may be derived from the plural suffix *-en*, and *-ger* is a noun indicator suffix which implies a person. Thus, *ämen'ger* refers to someone belonging to multiple families.

9. See *Shalghyn*, 1983, 1, pp. 89-112.

10. *Nawryz* corresponds to the month of March and, more specifically, refers to the New Year festival on the 22nd of March.

11. Zamzam is the site of a fountain, near Mecca.

12. The word *öltiri* is formed from *öl* (dead) and *tiri* (alive). Gifts which are given at this ceremonial occasion *(toi)* by the groom's side to the family of the bride, aside from livestock, include also pieces of fabric. White cloth is included in honor of the deceased ancestors of the girl's family.

13. Kazakh custom requires that a daughter-in-law, while approaching her father-in-law's family, should get down from her horse and walk the final stretch.

14. White sheep with yellow heads provide a positive omen.

15. A *zhelek* is a square scarf with tassled fringes. This scarf is the customary headdress of brides at Kazakh weddings.

Chapter 7

Fasting and Faith

The Kazakh expression of their Islamic faith is not limited to the special songs presented in this particular chapter. The attentive reader will have had no difficulty finding Islamic elements throughout this collection of Kazakh folk traditions. However, the songs which are gathered into this chapter are more explicitly Islamic; they pertain to the core of the Islamic religion—to fasting and to teaching.

Zharapazan Songs

Fasting is a sacred duty in many religions. Many faiths require or recommend fasting in one form or another during the calendar year, but ordinarily these admonitions pertain to very brief periods of time. Some religions forbid the consumption of certain tabu foods entirely, and restrict the consumption of other foods on specific days. For example, Han Chinese traditionalists refrain from eating meat on the first and fifteenth day of each month. With the introduction of Islam into China, followers of that religion subscribed, more or less, to abstinence from pork and to general fasting during Ramadan, the ninth lunar month, in accordance with the "five pillars".[1]

Ramadan is the month during which the holy Qur'an, according to its own testimony in Sura 2:185, was first sent down to Muhammad, by God. A month-long fast is held to commemorate this blessed event. No food, drink, or sexual relations are permitted from sunrise until sunset. This yearly observance of extended fasting, a rigid prayer schedule, and total abstinence from eating pork, are the most obvious practices that characterize the life styles of various denominations of Muslims in China.

Determined by the Muslim lunar calendar, the month of Ramadan travels through the entire solar year, and when it falls into the season of summer, the religious duty of abstinence from drink may be very demanding. People who weaken and lapse are expected to renew their vow to fast and to add an additional day of fasting beyond Ramadan. The only Muslims excused from this sacred duty are the sick, those who travel, mothers who are nursing infants, and small children.

If one considers the hardship of this month-long fast, it is not surprising if the new moon at the beginning of Shawwal—the tenth lunar month—is anxiously awaited. It signals the end of fasting and the celebration of Oraza Ait, or the Feast of Fast Breaking.[2] The feast lasts three days.

For this occasion every family prepares a variety of foods, and people ride on their horses wearing their best clothes. They wish their neighbors a happy feast. Specific Kazakh activities are being staged—horse races, *lakh tartyw*, and *khyz khuwar*.

Zharapazan songs—fast ending songs— are chanted when the new moon of Shawwal appears. Usually groups of boys gather outside the door of a yurt to sing. The heads of each family are expected to have gifts ready for the singers—usually some kind of food and boiled mutton. Wealthy families sometimes also give clothes to the singers, or even sheep and horses. The gifts which the singers receive are divided equally. Because gifts are given, some older singers like to join the group of boys to sing Zharapazan songs as well. Some even visit other families alone and sing solo.

The songs often begin with "In your family is one whom God *(Khudai)* loves."[3] The precise identity of the person who is divinely favored is usually left open for the listeners to guess. In any case, flattery and praise of the family and its possessions is aimed at convincing the head of a household to hand over more generously some gifts to the singers.

Your yurt, your yurt, is a beautiful yurt!
The beauty of your yurt depends on its stay-sticks.
The riches of your *saba* depends on your mares.[4]
The wealth of luggage depends on the strength of camels.
There is a yurt that looks like a white kingdom.
There are sheep that look like white antelopes.
That settlement is filled with happiness.
To which wealthy man does this yurt belong?
We were coming from that hill top,
Riding on stallions we came,
As they kept running they were difficult to rein,
Until we stopped here before your yurt of wealth.
From the high mountains and the low hills,
We came riding on strong bulls,
We could not stop them with nose ropes,
Until we came to yours, to a wealthy man's home.
May you be getting wealthier and wealthier!
Let misfortune be far away from you.[5]

After such initial songs of praise and blessing the actual Zhara-pazan or Fast-breaking Songs follow. These, then, remind and inform about the Five Pillars of Islam and confirm the Muslim faith. Each stanza is punctuated with a refrain that summarizes the purpose of the singing.

Assallawmaghalaikum! Peace be with you!
We come from a place where sun and moon rise.
We sing Zharapazan songs at midnight, be not offended!
The way of the Prophet we follow.
Refrain: Followers of Muhammad sing Zharapazan songs. It is *Oraza Ijman* that comes every twelve months.[6]

We sing Zharapazan songs for you, Bai.
The muezzin calls to prayer early in the morning.
To the singers of Zharapazan songs some gifts are due.
So you should not be punished in *Ahyret* (the Hereafter).[7]
    Refrain...

Are the people satisfied with the Zharapazan gifts?
Do people forsake their ancient traditions?
And if they abandon the ways of their ancestors,
Will they have a good life in Ahyret?
    Refrain...

Throughout your life do not do evil deeds.
Learn to pray five times a day.
If you do not pray five times a day,
No doubt, you will be drawn into hell (*tozakh*).
    Refrain...

We come to sing Zharapazan songs for your *awyl*.
You ought to give us clothes to wrap our bodies.
When you give us good clothes to wrap our waists,
We will praise you, and praise you, to our kin.
    Refrain...

We came to sing Zharapazan songs for your family.
Perhaps you prepared alms *(sadakha)* for us already.
Give a sheep, a lamb, we deem it not too much.
Rich harvests you will gather this year.
    Refrain...

Oraza comes once in twelve months.
Children of Muslims will gather.
If you give a horse to us, singers of Zharapazan,
Allah will give you much *sawab* (rectitude, equity).
    Refrain...

We come to sing Zharapazan songs for your family.
Dear Sister-in-law, bring out your gifts quickly.

If there are no gifts, no alms for us,
Our songs (of blessing) will not accompany you to Ahyret.
     Refrain....[8]

After the gifts have been handed to the singers, the oldest among
them will recite a blessing:

May the horses your children are riding
Be all gallopers!
While they are riding, galloping,
Let the heart of the master be content.
While you are looking at the moon (in the west),
While you are looking at the sun (in the east),
Let the silver pole of good fortune appear—
And your name be Sarybai.
On your beard is Sarymai.[9]
While on early mornings
The larks sing for you, always.
From the head of your bed,
From the end of your pillow,
The Khyzyr comes to protect you.
Be as a huge tree, full of branches.
Be full of light as our prophets.
Allahakpar!

Whereas originally the singing of Zharapazan songs was religiously
motivated, by a love for the tradition of Islam, the opportunity to obtain
gifts appears to have gradually distorted this original intent. Slight
humorous hints in the beginning, to the effect that small gifts would be
welcome and appropriate expressions of kindness, appear to have
deteriorated into bolder demands. The gap between the begging singers,
and the bai whom they flattered, appears to have widened in time.
Nevertheless, the distribution of gifts, together with the traditional
religious well-wishes and recited blessings, are precisely what helped
rich and poor to co-exist in peace.

I am coming here to see the moon.
I know this family is wealthier than all others.

Is that not an expression of their wealth—
I saw their cupboard full of butter.
    Refrain: Followers of Muhammad sing Zharapazan songs. It
is *Oraza Ijman* that comes every twelve months.

The red horse I rode under me is lame,
If you want to give one, make it a spirited one.
If you only give me a plate of cheese and a plate of butter,
I will regard these as a gold garment and a horse.
    Refrain...

We sing Zharapazan songs before your door.
May your son in the cradle be as strong as a ram.
And while your son grows strong as a ram,
Khudai (God) will watch over you.
    Refrain....

Sharyighat Songs

    The dissemination of the religion of Islam among the Kazakh
people was accomplished by way of reciting and composing poems.
Kazakh bards rearranged many Arabic and Persian folk tales into
poetry, and along the way their recitations became increasingly tinted
with the religious teachings and aspirations of Islam. Mullahs *(molda)*
to some extent imitated the styles of traditional bards who chanted epic
poetry. Muslim mullahs would recite their *Sharyjghat* songs to the
faithful on Fridays. Inasmuch as these recitations were heavily infused
with Arabic and some Persian words, the text of these songs was
usually not understood by the average Kazakh. Their Islamic meaning
was generally left to some mullah to expound.
    Sharyighat, derived from the Arabic *shari'a*, refers to "the way to
the water hole." It contains the meaning of the "right path" which one
is to follow in order to attain the goal of Islamic living. So it has come
to mean "Islamic Law." The general Kazakh purpose of "Sharyighat
songs" is to teach the rudiments of the way of Islam. The poem which
follows below demonstrates this intent.

The Kazakh Sharyighat song that follows here exists only in oral tradition. We found it cast in the form of a forbidding old dialect. On that account our recording in Kazakh/Arabic script had to be done phonetically first. The English translation was achieved by coordinating the thoughts of several scholars. It's rendition required knowledge of Kazakh, Arabic, Farsi, and a familiarity with Kazakh traditional ways—along with an extra ounce of editorial courage. This has been by far the most difficult document to include in this volume. Future generations of Kazakh linguists may come up with an improved translation some day. In order to increase this possibility we publish the words in the form of the Arabic script preferred by the Kazakhs themselves:

ءيا اللا حامدى ساننا كوپ ھيبه تلك ،
جارالعان اقوال - اقمر سيپاتلك .
حولكومك اللا اماد جانه ساماﺖ ،
وقىتشا توسىز ەشبىر مانگا ولوق زاتلك .
توماعان ، كوﯨدسوماعان بار دور ، بىر دور،
نازىل بوپ تالامكدا ملك ﯕبىراتلك .
ءالباجارا سوۇرەسىن اقوال بەرىپ ،
قورانذى وتىز پارا قىلدىك جاتىم .
بەرى - بمن سنسانلارىما پاپعامبار قمپ ،
ماككا مەن مەدينانلنك ۇالايتىن .
قاق جارىپ قارا قىلدان كون توعىز دلك،
مۇحاممەت مۇستافا دەپ اتلك اتىن .
ابۇباكىر ، وماسمەن موللا عۇسمان ،
مۇستاعان ۇالىي كەرەك مالىجاتىن .
وتىز جىلى مالىجالىق تامام بولىپ ،
اقىردا بۇزدى مورعان ناسيقاتىن .
اللانلك ون سەگىز ملك بالاسندا ،
پاپتاتى مەشجۇر لالامندا ،
ۇتىسنىپ مۇقتام بولماس ماعولىق بوق،
پيرى - بمن بەجۇىي كوننا س تامامندا .
قورىسمەتتى ول مويما سايىت عام ابرار،
ۇجماقتلك ورنى ۇارۇل ۇالاسندا .
مسعرابدىن وتىز خوامىپ بولدى عايان ،
بۇل تارتىپ اجىل ۇسلام اوابندا ،
اھ ۇرىپ ، خاغايىلا دەپ تامان ەتىپ،
سويلەپ توردون سالا غان قادامندا .

1. Oh Allah! You gave us everything.

2. From the beginning to end your workings are excellent.

3. Allah is the one and only God, the one and only God.

4. Great Allah, unlike anyone else, the only one.

5. Allah has not begotten nor has he been begotten.

6. We learned your name only from the Qur'an.

7. The Albahara sura was given first.

8. The Qur'an consists of thirty chapters.

9. You made prophets for angels, spirits, and humankind.[10]

10. All of them lived in Mecca and Medina.

11. You created a man just like the sun,

12. Who could split hairs into two fibers, Muhammad Mustafa.

13. Abu Bakr, Umar, Uthman

14. And Ali, these four may they reign forever.

15. After thirty years the caliphate system was broken.

16. Merwan destroyed that venerated tradition.

17. All kings on earth are created by Allah,

18. And everything that is mentioned in the Qur'an.

19. There is none who does not beg from the Almighty.

20. Including *peri, zhin,* and humankind.

21. He is guide for everyone.

22. He lives in heaven, a peaceful happy place.

23. One will know the thirty obligations *(wazhib)* from Heaven.

24. In early Islamic scriptures there are *wazhib.*

25. People are sighing and weeping,

26. At every step they sing ten eulogies.

بارا دى ٮٵٮكر الدنٮا قۇرٮلعان كۇن ،
قٮلعٮٮٮٮٮٮٮكٮ قادٮر اللٖا ساۇابٮندا .
عٵلٵمٮٮٮكٮ ۋٮن سٵگٮز مٮٮكٮ قٵق ٮٮٵرٮعٵرٮ ،
ٮۇٮرٵٮدى ٮمۇرك بٵلقٮٮٮٮ ٮٵ ٵلٮندا .
مۇ دٮ مٵلٵ سٮٮٮٮٮٮقٮن اٮٵٮ ٮٵزٮل ،
ٮٮان بولٵر مۇٮٮى اٮٮٮٵن ساۇابٮندا .
لٵۇلٵٮٵ ٮٮٵ ٮٵلانا مٵلٵقٮٮٮول اٮٮٮٵلٵٮٵ دٮٮپ ،
ٮٮٮر سۇٮٮٮكٮ بولدٮٮ ساۇابٮندا .
ٮنٮٮل ، ٮٵۇرٵٮ ، زابۇر سۇن مٵلٵم ٮٮٵرٵٮپ ،
ٮٮۇرٮ كٮٮٵٮٮ ۋٮٮلامى دٮۋٮدى ٮٵغٵبٮندا .
اٮٮٵٮٮٵن اٮٮٮلٵٮٮن پٵٮٵٵ سٮٵرٮٵر ،
قٵرٮق ٮٮٮٮلٮٮون ، ۋٮ ٮٮٵ ٮٮٵن ٮٵٮٵ ٵرٮٵرٮٵر ،
ۇٮٮٮٮٮى سۇكٮٮون سٮٮٮٮ ، ٮۇرٮ مٵزٵ ٮٮٮ ن
ۇ ٮٵ قٮٵ دٮ ٮٮ سٮٮٮٮٮن مدرسٮ بٵر ،
ٮٮٵٮٵرٮن بٵٮٮٮٮول مٵ مٮٮول ٮٮرٮٮٮٮٮ الٮٵن ،
مۇقٵ دٮ ٮ سٮ كۇٮٮٮرٮٮٮٮٮ ٮٮٵرٵٮ قٵلٮٵن .
ٮٮٮٮٮٮٮٮ كٮٮٮٮٮٮٮكٮ ٮۇٮم پٵٮٵٵ سٮٵرٮ ،
قٵۇٮٮٵ ۋٮ سٵگٮز مٮٮكٮ ۋسٮٮٵم سٵلٮٵن

27. After each step they praise ten times.

28. After (life in this world) people will go to God *(Tängri)*

29. And beg Almighty Allah to forgive them.

30. You are the guide for everybody.

31. From your face light is shining.

32. Sincere rules are in your book.

33. Obedient people will be blessed by you.

34. By your command there is this world and humankind.

35. Enzhil, Täwrät, Zäbir, and Qur'an.

36. There are answers in these four books.

37. We honor the prophets.

38. We have forty *shilten*, twelve imams, and four caliphs.[11]

39. Eighty *seits* are divided into four divisions.[12]

40. Idris with his body is in Heaven.[13]

41. Baitul Maghmul has been moved to Heaven.

42. Sacred places *(mukaddes)* were left on earth,

43. All things in Noah's boat,

44. Became the origin of all things later.[14]

Notes

1. The five pillars or foundational precepts of Islam are: (1) The profession of faith "there is no God but Allah and Muhammad is the messenger of Allah." (2) Prayer, performed five times daily—morning, noon, mid-afternoon, sunset, and evening. (3) Almsgiving to the poor. (4) Fasting during the month of Ramadan. (5) Making a pilgrimage to Mecca, if physically and financially able.
2. *Oraza Ait* (Breaking of the Fast at the end of Ramadan) is one of two major Muslim holidays, the other being *Qurban Ait* (Feast of Sacrifice.)

3. *Khudai* in Kazakh is derived from the Persian *Huda*. Along with the Arabic designation *Allah*, this is a name for God.

4. A *saba* is a huge bag, made of horse skin, which holds twenty to thirty liters of khymyz—fermented mare's milk.

5. Mukhtar Äwezov, *Collected Works*, vol. 16, pp. 46-47. Alma Ata: Writers' Publishing House of Kazakhstan, 1985.

6. "Muhammet, ümbet aitkhan zharapazan. Bir kelgen on eki aida oraza ijman." *Oraza ijman* refers to the faith of *Oraza ait*, the annual feast that celebrates breaking the fast at the end of Ramadan. The faith of that holy day is, of course, the same as the faith of the "first pillar" (see Note 1) or first duty of Islam.

7. *Ahyret* means Hereafter, the Other World, or the Netherworld. The same word also refers to the white linen shroud into which the dead are wrapped.

8. This and the following two songs were collected by Awelkhan Hali during winter of 1960, in Buwryltoghai county, Altai prefecture, Xinjiang.

9. The rhyme of *sarymai* (butter) and the name of a man, *Sarybai* (Yellow-Rich-One), plays as well on "yellowness" as on the richness of butter.

10. The Kazakh word *peri* pertains to female celestials or angels, *zhin* means spirits or deamons, and *insan* refers to humankind.

11. "Forty *shilten*" are forty Arab men who brought Islam to Xinjiang, they were killed in battle and buried there.

12. Eighty female descendants of the prophet Muhammad.

13. The quranic Idris corresponds to the biblical Enoch.

14. Collected by the authors from Beisenghalyi, a nomadic herder in Dörbilzhin County, of the Tarbaghatai Prefecture of Xinjiang, 1988.

Chapter 8

The Legacy of Ancient Shamanism

In the course of their evolution the Kazakh people have subscribed to a variety of religious ways. First there was shamanism and primitive herder religion, then Buddhism, Nestorian Christianity, and now their religiosity is defined mostly by Islam. It appears that Islam made inroads among the Kazakhs during the 10th Century. A visitor to Kazakhland should keep in mind, nevertheless, that Islam there is defined, still today, more by pastoralism as a way of life than by an institutionalized religious tradition. Inasmuch as many Kazakh nomads to this day have not yet established permanent residences for themselves, they also have learned to make do with fewer mosques and with less formal religious instruction. If Kazakh religiosity today were to be compared with that of other Islamic peoples in China, such as the more sedentary Hui, the Islam of the Kazakhs would appears less well established.

While the Kazakh people subscribe to Islam perhaps earnestly enough, they cultivate at the same time customs that are still solidly rooted in more ancient ways of Central Asiatic herder existence. But whatever the roots of their contemporary customs, their level of religiosity has served them as a unifying magnet throughout the better part of our millennium.

Shamanism Surviving

Shamanism is an ancient way of relating to the world which existed already during the Stone Age, four and more thousands of years ago. It still embraces elements from the religion and the cultural level of ancestral Stone Age hunters. Shamanic healers and practitioners have survived in much of northern Europe and Asia, as well as in aboriginal America.

The ancestors of present-day Kazakh people have been living in Central and Western Asia since prehistoric times. During those long millennia the world view of shamanism has dominated their thinking, their work and their culture. It has shaped their mythology and folklore, their customs, their material culture and their arts. It was the shamans who established contact with Heaven on high, who maintained that contact between gods and humankind, and who mediated the blessings of Heaven unto the earth.

In the Kazakh language a shaman is called a *"bakhsy,"* a word borrowed from Mongolian. The Mongolian word *"bakhchi"* nowadays refers to a person of virtue, such as a teacher. The modern adaptation of this term is appropriate inasmuch as prehistoric hunter bands did not yet differentiate between shamanic activities and teaching. A shaman in archaic hunter traditions has simply been the intellectual leader of a group of hunters.

In ancient days shamans *(bakhsy)* played prominent roles in the everyday affairs of the nomadic Kazakh people. Even today it appears as though sometimes the shamanic tasks of divination and healing, among Kazakh herdsmen, are more important than the service of mullahs. As they have before the advent of Islam, Kazakhs still today regard their shamans as agents of eternal Heaven, or as messengers of Heaven. A shaman has the reputation of seeing everything more clearly than other people. He knows everything between high Heaven and the Netherworld, and he knows as well how to interact and interfere in these extreme realms. He is a poet, a musician, a healer, and he knows how to induce trance. While in trance, a shaman today still contacts gods, and God, with the assistance of his traditional helper spirits. He contacts gods which, meanwhile by Islam, have become redefined as angels. A shaman influences what modern outsiders would rather recognize as being forces of nature. He summons wind and rain, and he drives away diseases.

Even though the practice of shamanism still continues in the shadows of Kazakh society, information about it is difficult to obtain nowadays. Representatives and leaders of Islam have through the centuries been not too kindly disposed toward these shamanic retainers of heathenism. Moreover, in the course of the twentieth century, Kazakh shamans have periodically been persecuted because their archaic ways did not seem to be in step with ideological styles of modernity that happened to be in vogue. Persecution of traditionalists happened especially during the decade of the so-called Cultural Revolution. The fact remains that until now neither Buddhism, Islam, nor Marxist modernity have been able to understand or satisfy all the physical, intellectual, and spiritual needs of typical Central Asiatic nomadic herders.

Akhatai was a shaman who was active during the 1940s in one of the northern Kazakh regions in Xinjiang. In 1988 we were fortunate to have obtained a reliable eye witness account from one of his apprentices. When Akhatai shamanized he wore special attire. His garment and trousers were made of red velvet. Strips fringed with tassels were hanging from the rim of his round hat *(takhyja)*. To the shoulders of his outer garment owl feathers were stitched, and an amulet hung around his neck. Usually he held in his hand a decorated stick, a wand, which he used during his proceedings.

In one instance Akhatai was asked to cure a woman who suffered from mental disorientation. The shaman agreed and came to the patient's yurt. First he asked the master of the yurt to hang a piece of red cloth outside the door, and then he requested that the patient wash herself. After that he ordered that two cauldrons be set up. One of these was filled with sheep fat, and the other with water, and both together were brought to a boil. Into the fire he placed seven kinds of metal implements—an axe, a shovel, a sickle, a knife, a hoe, an iron bowl, and a cartridge shell.

After everything was ready, the shaman asked that the patient be called in, and he began to play his dombra to a tune of Khorkhyt.[1] As the intensity of the song increased, the shaman himself began to sweat and to tremble. He began to work himself into a trance and invoked his helping spirits, his *zhin*, by lamentingly calling the name "Sarkhashykh."[2]

Every Kazakh shaman has his helper spirits, and most of these spirits are monstrous personages—such as Kökpar the blue deity, Pushyk the nose deity, Zhalpakh Tanaw the flat-nose deity. Some helper spirits appear much like ordinary animals and plants, such as the gray wolf, the yellow bitch, the white horse, or various kinds of trees.

After a while, Akhatai the shaman confessed that his helper spirit was not forthcoming. This meant that he was unable to cure the patient. In response some old people who were present implored: "Oh, our Reverend One! Please speak some words of good fortune *(akh söjle)*, and Allah will give you long life."

Then the shaman, holding a staff in his hand, walked around the patient, first clockwise and then counter-clockwise. He chanted *bakhsy* songs as he went. When his song neared a climax he worked himself into a state of frenzy and ecstacy. He took a ladle and sprinkled hot water at the yurt walls in all directions. He picked up felt pieces and put them into the boiling sheep fat, and after that he burned them. From the fire he removed the knife and stabbed against his own chest—the blade bent. He took out the axe and hacked against his chest—he felt no pain. He took out the shovel and stepped on it—he did not feel a burning sensation. He took out the hoe and licked it with his tongue; he took out the iron bowl and held it in his hands; he took out the sickle and hung it around his neck. And with none of these feats was he himself injured. At last he took out the cartridge shell and put it into his mouth.

After having done all these things the people who were present admired him and believed in him. Then he strode toward the sick woman who was lying there. Soon thereafter the patient fell asleep.

On the next day the shaman spat cold water at the patient, and she was restored to health.

One of Akhatai's songs went as follows. It has been learned and remembered by one of the participants:

My name is Akhatai, the *bakhsy.*
From my elders I have received blessings *(bata).*
Compared to men of my age, my disposition is gentle.
I am as wide as the earth.
Allah! You let me suffer torments which I should not.
Allah! Let me beg this withered twig (his wand).

Yellow Bitch, pass by here!
Come, my Helper Spirit!
O my Blue Helper Spirit, come, my Helper Spirit!
O my Bull Camel! O Bull Camel!
Come quickly as I call you, though your nose is flat!
Yellow Bitch!
Hey, Flat Nose with two humps!

Hey, Hat worn on my head![3]
Allah! You let me suffer torments which I should not.
Allah! Let me beg this withered twig.
O Allah! Have mercy on me, mercy on me.
Give power to the religion of Islam.
I beg You, save this patient.
Let him (her) be cured, restored to health![4]

The empowerment of shamans does not happen through a gradual acquisition of skills or hypnotic healing powers. A shaman knows that on a specific day, in the course of a specific year, a certain spirit helper has associated itself with him. Akhatai began to shamanize at age seventeen. The above quoted verses indicate that he called three spirit helpers—Yellow Bitch, Blue Deity, and Bull Camel. At the same time, it is not inconceivable that all three of these appellation were the names of a single spirit helper.

Along with the shaman's divine resources we have also seen how Akhatai has begun his song with apologetically portraying himself as "gentle." Moreover, he has made an honest attempt to wrap himself into the tradition of Islam. Akhatai's prayers to Allah reach far beyond defensive apologetics and societal justification of his activities. He attributed the very torments of his occupation, thus his entire calling of being a shaman, to the initiative of Allah. He hoped to use his shamanic wand with Allah's endorsement. By way of the religion of Islam, all his spirit helpers derived their powers from Allah. In the end it was Allah, the God of Heaven, who was asked to save the patient—no longer the traditional helper spirits, or a living Heaven *(Tängri)* that, Islamically speaking, is seen reduced to a place that serves as Allah's abode.

From shamanic proceedings reported elsewhere in Kazakhland it appears that the procedures of other shamans are similar. There are only differences in detail. Some shamans hold no wands in their hands. Some invite people to be present while they shamanize, whereas others go into hiding to maintain an air of mystery. Some used seven kinds of iron tools, while others utilized five or nine varieties.

The notion of Heaven being the supreme deity is not something that needed to be introduced into Kazakh shamanism by the way of Islam. Blue Heaven *(Kök Tängri)*, or simply Heaven *(Tängri)*, has been recognized as the principal supreme deity by Kazakhs and other Central Asiatic herder tribes all along. It is solidly documented in pre-Islamic mythos and ethos, and in Kazakh epics as well. Take for instance an excerpt from a still popular epic poem.

> If a knife is not sharp it may cut your hand,
> But it cannot cut the red willow.
> A fixed world is difficult to change
> If the banner falls.
> A stallion and a spay,
> The patient's relatives will offer.
> And oh, if Heaven does not relent,
> The patient will have to go with Him.[5]

And consider this next passage from "Khabekeng":

> The hero Khabanbai from Baitalakh clan,
> A horse I have readied for you.
> Khabekeng's spirit will help you.[6]
> Whether our tribe will be safe, or not,
> We ask our ancestral spirits to help us.[7]
> I put iron into the fire
> And lick it again and again,
> To drive diseases far away.
> I take out the iron burned,
> I step on it with my foot.
> I spit water with my mouth.
> Has a pit been dug?
> Is there a fire burning with rage?

If there are diseases in our tribe,
Let me drive them away.

Khara Kerei, Khabanbai,
Khazhyghaly, Bögenbai!
O hero Zhänyibek, how ill I feel![8]
I cannot find a way to cure my sickness.
My White Spirit and Blue Spirit,
While I call on you, come quickly.
I hope you help me find a way.
Bring that way to my hand, give it to me.
I feel unwell, my Yellow (Male) Dog,
A voice you have given me,
I now see everything more clearly.
I see everything even in dark night.
O my White Spirit, do not go away!
O my Blue Spirit, do not leave me alone![9]

Invocations

The procedures of shamanic practitioners do not always remain under their exclusive professional jurisdiction. The masses of people learn from their intellectual leaders what they can and practice what seems useful. Thus, invocations that request rain, or conjurations to expel snake venom, have traditionally been used by ordinary people as well. All these practices may be considered under the heading of "Invocations" or *Arbaw*. The word *arbaw* means to invoke and to lure, to conjure, to seduce, and to mediate.

Rain requesting by way of reciting poetic invocations is a remnant of ancient shamanic practices; it still reflects the world view and culture level of early domesticators. Natural forces, back then, were still perceived as nature persons who thought and acted. Therefore, spoken language, similar to that which facilitated communication among persons in human society, was used to communicate with greater-than-human nature persons. The ancients communicated with various aspects of nature in human words. They interacted with and reasoned about these greater realities. Gradually they learned to persuade, and later to conquer portions of these realities experimentally. But before they began to experiment and to control arrogantly and scientifically, they used the more polite approach of invocations.

During droughts the ancient Kazakhs assembled along rivers and mountain slopes to sacrifice black goats. They cooked the meat of these goats, recited invocations, chanted rain-requesting songs, and ate the meat during a communal meal. They begged Heaven and Earth to prevent disaster and to provide good fortune. Here are some examples of prayers addressed to clouds:

> White clouds are like the heads of horses,
> Blue clouds are like the heads of sheep.
> Reeds have dried up along the lakes,
> Fall heavy, Rain, we beg you!
> White Clouds, you are our friends and life,
> Let us be soaked to the skin, o Clouds!
>
> Gray Clouds, with gentle breezes,
> Do not make us impatient. Rain quickly!
> Come! Come Clouds! Come!
> You are the offspring of two mothers.[10]
> You are rolling faster than the floods of rivers,
> Come Clouds—come on rolling and floating![11]

Another kind of prayer aims at removing venom that had been injected by a serpent's fangs. To ask the clouds to drop rain does amount to invocative polite begging; by contrast, the prayer that follows next, for the removal of snake poison, is an exercise in scolding—it is undisguised exorcism. While exorcistic prayers are being recited, with grave seriousness, the serpent who has bitten a person or a domestic animal is visualized as lying unconscious. With the originator of the venom being laid low in this manner, and rendered inactive, the effects of injected poison can be reversed more easily:

> Arrogant, arrogant, arrogant Serpent!
> Biting Serpent with triangular head!
> There is a serpent, a rude serpent,
> There is a serpent, a dark-brown serpent,
> There is a serpent who has not given birth seven years![12]
> Frightened you come from Khuralai Mountain,
> You brood of crafty serpents.

Paighambars are throwing holy water on the patient;
They command that the venom will be quickly removed.[13]

The recitation of prayer-incantations for the removal of serpentine venom illustrates that the people believe in the persuasive power of human commands against the world's nonhuman or superhuman personages. This is an ancient way. And to this very day old Kazakh people think that serpents have their own language, that those who understand this language can communicate with them. Some old men even insist that on some occasions during the course of their lives, they have seen certain people converse with serpents. But from the quoted conjuration one may also conclude that effective commands are nowadays no longer explained in terms of ancient shamanism, but in terms of Islam. Prophets of Allah are now the ones who sprinkle healing water and accomplish some kind of exorcistic catharsis—as well as offer encouragement to get well.

Chants to Cure *Bädik*

Bädik is a disease which affects cattle. Its symptoms cannot be defined with precision, because *bädik* also has become a general designation for any "disease" that affects livestock as well as humankind.

Back in ancient times, the Kazakh shamans knew different gods (superhuman causes and curers) of the different diseases. Occasionally one still finds a traditional shamanic song that was intended for use by an individual keeper of horses:

Delbe comes to the horses.[14]
It is a disease seldom heard of.
We hope that in our life
We never encounter a disease like this.
Horses are biting each other,
Are neighing on the wastelands.
When you lead them they will not move.
Sometimes they lead you to the *zheli*.[15]
They do not eat grass well.
They do not drink water well.

We beg Allah to dispel this disease.
Let *delbe* leave us and go far away![16]

Singing *bädik* songs such as this may be accompanied by a variety of activities. A sick horse is usually covered with blankets. Then, the man who sings this song may walk the sick horse in a circle around the *zheli* place—the place identified with the youthfulness of horses. Sometimes a sick horse is walked between two stacks of fire. Sometimes it is led to an ancestor's grave to remain there for the night. And occasionally, entire herds of cattle afflicted by an epidemic are driven at night to the graves of ancestors to find reprieve. Sometimes a rope is stretched between two trees, and to that rope a copy of the Qur'an is tied. Sick horses are then made to walk under the rope between the two trees; *bädik* songs are chanted all the while. Such practices show that today the Kazakh people occasionally still reason after the manner of their ancient shamans, that they respect fire and revere their ancestors, and that on top of it all, for good measure, they practice Islam.

The shamanic practice of singing *bädik aitys* (bädik songs) has become popularized when young people were brought in to participate in the healing rituals. Bonfires were built at night, and *bädik aitys* were chanted antiphonally by boys and girls. The initial purpose was, clearly enough, to expel disease.

Antiphonal singing was done by young people—by boys who represented an entire *awyl* or settlement. They surrounded the sick animal which did lie at the center. On one side stood the boys, and the girls stood opposite. One side, in unison, called attention to the problem and the other side responded. It seems as though the presence of these young people—all this youthfulness and vigor—was intended to exude health unto the sick animals. They always began with the exclamation *Kösh!* and thereby they demanded movement.

Boys:
 Kösh! Kösh![17]
 When we sing *bädik* songs, we always start with this.
 All of us wear clothes made of velvet,
 We see it lie there, not eating grass, not drinking water.
 If this is not *bädik*, then what is it?

> *Kösh! Kösh!*

Girls:

> *Kösh! Kösh!*
> The disease is going away, you see, going far away.
> I take the bridle and run to the horse.
> God bless me so I can capture the *bädik* with my hands,
> So I can throw it into the bonfire!
> *Kösh! Kösh!*

Boys:

> *Kösh! Kösh!*
> Drive the diseases deep into the mountains!
> Drive them to the rapid stream!
> *Kösh! Kösh!*

Girls:

> *Kösh! Kösh!*
> Drive them into the whirlwind!
> Drive them to the serpents and scorpions!
> *Kösh! Kösh!*[18]

In the course of Kazakh history the practice of antiphonal *bädik* singing has lost some its original meaning and function. Young people, once they were permitted to gather on a good pretext, had more things on their minds than merely to heal sick animals. Nowadays young people, boys and girls, still gather for antiphonal singing to dance and to sing love songs—in the same antiphonal style. In fact, there is an antiphonal song which itself explains this pretext and change of purpose:

Girls:

> *Bädik* singings are a good pretext to get together.
> Please come to our *awyl* and sing antiphonal songs at night.
> *Bädik* singings can be a pretext for all of us.
> I can find a way to meet with you.

Boys:

> My Black Mountains! My Black Mountains!
> Black winds are blowing from the mountain tops.

We know that in your house is a *bädik*.
Our *awyl* is moving downhill.[19]

The pretext is in earnest and complete. The girls are calling and
the boys are responding. And, in this context the word *bädik* chanted
by the boys no longer means "disease." It refers to the "heart," or to
their "love" of a girl.

Notes

1. See Khongyrtbajev Ä. "Khazakh Folklorynyng Tarijhy," in *Ana Tili*
(Mother Tongue), 1991, pp. 86f. *Khorkhyt Ata* is a famous bard *(akhyn)*,
composer, and actor who lived during the 9th or 10th Century. He is known
as the father of Turkic music. His tunes are mostly sorrowful laments.
2. *"Sarkhashykh"* literally means "Yellow Bitch." It was Akhatai's helping
spirit.
3. In Kazakh tradition even an ordinary hat represents an important dimension
of the bearer's personality.
4. Collected from Zhekebai, a nomadic herder, in Toly County, Tarbaghatai
Prefecture, 1988.
5. Collected from Beisenghaly, a nomadic herder, in Dörbilzhin County,
Tarbaghatai Prefecture, 1988.
6. *Khabekeng* is the name of a Kazakh national hero of the 18th Century. It is
a nickname for *Khabanbai* that signifies endearment.
7. During battle, horse races, and wrestling matches Kazakh people shout the
names of their forefathers, or the names of heroes of their tribe.
8. Khara Kerei and Khazhyghaly are tribal names. Bögenbai and Zhänyibek are
heroes of the 18th Century.
9. Collected from a Kazakh nomadic herder in Shaweshek County, Tarbaghatai
prefecture, Xinjiang, in 1988. Name withheld upon request.
10. The two mothers of the clouds are Heaven and Earth.
11. Collected from Khudym, a nomadic herder in Sawan County, Tarbaghatai
Prefecture, Xinjiang, in 1988.
12. These three lines add up to scolding the hostile serpent. The dark-brown
color signifies fearsomeness, and "seven years of infertility" amount to an
insult or a curse.

13. Collected from Zhekebai, Toly County, Tarbaghatai prefecture, Xinjiang, in 1988. *Paighambars* are prophets or messengers of Allah. To remove an illness, Kazakh mullahs usually sprinkle purifying water on the faces and chests of their patients.

14. The symptoms of *delbe* are that horses bite each other at their necks and backs.

15. *Zheli* specifically refers to the rope stretched between pegs to tie up young animals. It is the place where the offspring of horses is kept.

16. Collected from Äniwar, in Shasha, ca. 47 kilometers from Shäweshek city, Xinjiang, in 1988.

17. *Kösh!* is the exorcistic command which means "Get away!" "Get out!" "Move away!"

18. See Anonymous. *Istoria Kazakskoi Literatury* (*History of Kazakh Literature*) 1, pp. 110-113, Alma Ata: Academy Publishing House of Kazakhstan, 1960.

19. Collected from Äniwar, in Shasha, ca. 47 kilometers from Shäweshek city, Xinjiang, in 1988.

Chapter 9

In the Dimension of Time

The Calendar Year

Calendars are an invention that helped early domesticators obtain handles on the processes of change—on time passing. While our modern Western calendar, and our reckoning of months and weeks, still abounds in references to divinized emperors and ancient gods, the Kazakh calendar reflects a still more ancient reckoning of the flow of time. Essentially theirs is the Chinese calendar which has been a creation of domesticators. It has been constructed on the basis of animal categories, a mode of thinking that derives from the still more ancient hunter-gatherer stratum of human culture. The Kazakh calendar, like the Chinese, counts twelve years toward a larger cycle. Within each twelve-year cycle, specific years are named after animals in the following sequence: Rat, Cow, Tiger, Hare, Dragon, Snake, Horse, Sheep, Monkey, Hen, Dog, and Pig. Along with the Kazakhs, other Altaic peoples such as the Mongols, Daghur, Sibe, and others farther east, also have adopted this Chinese calendar. The identification of specific years within twelve year cycles, by way of marking each year with a memorable animal, makes it relatively easy to figure some-one's age or to calculate a moment's distance from past historical events.

There are many Kazakh legends that rationalize the Chinese calendar—that explain why certain animals are used to designate certain

179

years, or why a twelve-year cycle begins with the "Year of the Rat."
What follows here is a story that attempts to Islamicize the presence of
the Chinese "pig" in the Kazakh calendar. The story also explains the
embarrassing fact why the Islamically more important camel is absent.
The fact that Kazakhs have adopted a non-Islamic Chinese calendar is
not admitted or confronted directly.

> Once upon a time it was announced that the year was coming.
> None of the animals knew whether it would bring good or bad
> luck. They therefore gathered to welcome the year. Each of them
> wanted to be first in seeing the new year arrive, and so they
> started quarrelling. Camel did not worry because it had a long
> neck and therefore was taller than the others. When all of them
> stood there, waiting for the year to arrive, the Rat climbed up on
> the Camel's head and clung to the tip of its ear. While the others
> still had not seen the new year come, Rat shouted: "I saw it
> coming, and I am the first!" Camel became angry and began
> chasing the rat. And while Camel was absent, the other animals
> saw the year arrive in the forementioned order. In this manner, the
> years were named beginning with Rat, and Camel was left out.[1]

Poetry is the means by which Kazakh adults taught their children
how to memorize the Chinese twelve year calendar:

> An animal that is an enemy of humankind,
> It steals and eats grain, makes you go hungry.
> But it enters the sequence of years firstly.
> If you do not know, please remember, its name is Rat.

> Another animal that is fat during winter and summer,
> The people like its meat and milk.
> The people old and young give it the name of a year.
> If you do not know, please remember, its name is Cow.

> An animal that lives in deep forests,
> Lives far away from you and does not give you a glimpse.
> But it also came to a year, like others.
> If you do not know, please remember, its name is Tiger.

An animal whose ears are as long as a pine tree,
Not a piece of fat can be found anywhere on its body.
But it also enters a year, like others.
If its name is not Hare, what else could it be?

An animal that lives in deep pools,
And though (some) people have seen it they never minded,
It also came to a year to add its name.
If you do not know it, its name is Dragon.[2]

An animal that moves along as water flows,
Has no arms and no legs and is special,
But it also enters a year, like others.
If you do not know, please remember, its name is Snake.

Red foxes are playing along mountain slopes,
To hunt them is a game of fun.
Your companion (in that game) enters the year from there.
If you do not know, please remember, its name is Horse.

You slaughter an animal when guests come to your house,
That animal slaughtered is usually a sheep.
Remember its name and never forget—
Sheep is the name of the eighth year.

An animal that seems more clever than man,
Yet people say it is a degeneration.
While it comes to a year, no-one knows its real name.
People wrote it down as *Meshin*.[3]

It is a bird, but it cannot fly,
People found and tamed and trained it.
If you do not know, please remember.
Its name is Hen, and comes to the tenth year.

An animal that lives by livestock shelters,
It is a diligent guardian through day and night.
If you do not know, please remember,
Its name is Dog and occupies the eleventh year.

An animal that is different from others, and looks ugly.
Some people love it as much as their other animals.
If you do not know, its name is Pig.
Even though it is tabu *(haram)*, it occupies a year.[4]

The Celebration of New Year

The Kazakh word *nawryz* is derived from the Persian word *nawruz,* which means "New Year." The beginning of a new year has been celebrated by many peoples in Asia. It has been a festival for sedentary as well as nomadic peoples, such as the Turks, Kazakhs, Uighurs, Uzbeks, and Kirghiz. Since ancient times it also has been a tradition among Arabs.

The survival and livelihood of peoples in the temperate zone are very much dependent on the cycles and seasons in nature. Winter to the Central Asiatic nomads is a burdensome season. With the great temperature differences that occur near the center of the world's largest land area, the cold season brings many hardships whereas the summer, by contrast, is a time of plenty of melt-water and lush grass. During summer the herd animals grow strong, and the lives of their nomadic owners become more secure. The people therefore regard spring time as the beginning of a new year.

The majority of Central Asiatic nomads celebrate New Year at the beginning of spring, that is, during the spring equinox of the solar year, when daytime and nighttime are equal. The Kazakhs have determined the 21st or 22nd of March to be their New Year festival, and they refer to it as *"ulystyng ulys küni"* which means "the first great day of the year."

Historically, this Kazakh folk festival has not been directly derived from their practice of Islam. According to ancient Chinese historical records about the western regions of present-day Xinjiang, the Kazakh and Uighur people have been celebrating New Year already at the time of the Tang dynasty (618-907 C. E.). Male and female, old and young, celebrated the New Year festival. They sang and danced from sunset until the next morning. By these activities they sought to expel, to heal and to ward off such things as grief, illness, wounds, epidemics, death, devils, evil spirits, demons, enemies and misfortunes.

From these clues we can infer, with reasonable certainty, that the Kazakh people have had a long history of celebrating their *nawryz*. But then, by adapting here and there a little to the different life styles of neighboring peoples with whom they merged, by adopting agriculture and handicrafts to supplement their pastoralism, the festival has lost some of its former meanings. Nevertheless, to the extent that pastoral nomadism remains still the time-honored Kazakh way, their New Year festival remains a strong tradition all the while.

At the New Year festival most Kazakh families cook *nawryz közhe*, a kind of gruel made of rice, millet, wheat, cheese, meat, salt, and water. Groups of people can be seen emerging from one *awyl,* travelling to visit their friends in another. The host family prepares gruel for the guests, they sing *nawryz* verses while embracing one another warmly. They speak good wishes for each other and for their new year:

"May the first great day be lucky;
  Ulys bakhytty bolsyn;
May your milk be plentiful;
  Tört tülik akhty bolsyn;
Where you go may your journey be safe;
  Khaida barsa, zhol bolsyn;
May all misfortunes be buried into the earth!
  Bäle zhala zherge ensin![5]

The song of a girl lamenting the death of her father—still popular today—sheds indirect light on the meaning with which Kazakh people have endowed the celebration of their New Year:

Oh! My dear Papa,
Why did you marry me to a poor man?
No matter how much brains he has—
Are not even poor people saying he is a poor man?

If you had married me to a rich man, Papa,
Then on this great New Year festival,
I would butcher a stallion with fat a span thick.
I would butcher a sheep with fat a span thick.
On this festival day, why should I not butcher?

Poor people could then have a good meal,
And it could light up a couple of lamps as well.

Poems such as these testify to the fact that Kazakh people were accustomed to butchering their best livestock to entertain their New Year guests, and they performed special rites to celebrate New Year. The "couple of lamps," here, are New Year lamps and have reference to the greater *Tängri* as "Heaven" and "Fire." They refer to veneration of Heaven and Fire.

Additional practices are associated with the Kazakh New Year celebration. All chipped wooden bowls and spoons are broken, they are thrown away or burned. Such defective things are remnants of the year that passed. It is assumed that old imperfections carried over into the new year could bring misfortune to their owners. While breaking or burning these things, invocative and conjurative words are repeated over and again:

"Welcome, welcome New Year! Come to us, new happiness! Roll away, Misfortune *(Khairaghan)!*"

In short, the people take leave from last year's disasters and misfortunes, so that these or their likenesses might never return. They hope for, and they welcome, a year that is completely fresh and new. To that effect, when people meet each other on that day, they express their regards approximately as follows:

"Are you well? May Ulys (the New Year festival day) make you successful!"

"May there be plenty of milk, and may it be well wherever you go!"

"May Ulys make you rich!"

"May misfortunes disappear into the earth!"

Elders express their respects toward young people by way of reciting similar blessings or invocations:

"God bless us!"

"Come, New Happiness, come!"

"Our Owner-God! May everything turn out as we hope!"

"Move, move away, Misfortune! I never want to see you again!"

Along with speaking short greetings, special songs are chanted and poems are recited during the New Year celebration:

If at Ulys our buckets are full,
That whole year will yield milk aplenty.
If you ask a blessing from a great man,
You will win many trophies.

On the great Ulys day,
The wealthy man *(bai)* comes forth and feels happy.
Next to him stands his daughter,
Braids are draping down over her breasts.

The bai's wife comes forth, plump in figure,
The edge of her scarf keeps the sunlight off her face.
His daughter-in-law emerges, proudly proud,
Their colorful scarfs touch and make tingling sounds.[6]

The bai's daughter emerges, shyly shy.
Her eyes are shiny bright.
Male slaves hurry through work routines like antelopes,
They have escaped from sticks and whips this day.

Female slaves have avoided sticks and whips as well.
Defective spoons and bowls are burned,
Billowing smoke and flames are rising.[7]

The cheerful and happy mood of the New Year celebration is emphasized still further as the people wear their newest clothes. Even the poor, and the slaves (male *khul* and female *khung*) in ancient times, have rejoiced on that festival day. They left behind the old, burned or discarded what was old and imperfect, and welcomed a new state of happiness and wellbeing.

From Youth to Old Age

Once the calendar was structured, to the extent that it made sense comfortably within a world of herders and animals, the human mind could again relax and return from the concern of "time passing" to the business of how to "pass the time." With a measure of tranquility the human mind can muse about the aging process to which all life on earth is subjected. There never is a time when human misfortunes are not at least a little bit funny—at least in the perspective of those who momentarily are riding on a spree of good luck.

Songs about different age levels depict changes in physiological stature and behavior, also changes that occur in one's mode of thinking. Generally, five to ten years is considered an age level. Songs about different age levels are sung at reunions and other joyous occasions. Getting older by necessity while at the same time desiring to remain young, and being hampered by awkward behavior that results from this time lag of desire in the human mind, is indeed something to laugh about.

Ages always start from one.
Let me sing a song about ages, do not be in a hurry.
At that time (age one) mother's milk is food.
There is no need to drink from other pots.

When one starts talking one's age is two.
Though at that time the words are not clear.
One has a spoon and a bowl,
But one still wants to fetch food from the elders.

From four or five onward he starts playing,
One runs barefoot huffing and puffing.
Without provocation he pouts his lips,
And childishly he has no esteem for the elders.

At ten he is still the pet of his parents,
Is still the apple of their eyes, their Dear One.
All faults are still counted toward his childlike nature,
Which can be considered neither good nor bad.

At fifteen he jumps from here to there like a kid,
Riding on a foal or a calf without saddle.
O that early youth—it never returns—
This carefree way of acting like a spoiled child.

At fifteen she looks as bright as the moon,
Like a foal sucking the nibbles of two mares.
Even if you dash your head against rocks,
O that age fifteen, it never returns.

The age of twenty is an active time,
His temperament gets easily excited, like a bull in heat
With an older bull joining the fun,
When he sees girls, young ladies laugh and joke on end.

At twenty-five he dresses up,
He shaves his face every day.
He takes his older brothers as models,
Loafing from dawn to dusk, getting thinner each day.

Thirty is the age for play.
He is not satisfied with peak excitement or fun.
He marries a woman to bear a child, he tends his livestock.
He thinks about working for his family.

Thirty-five is a ripe age for a man,
Is the age to blossom and bear fruit.
If he is a lad with great ability,
Happiness and good fortune go to his head.

Age forty, it is said, is (as sharp as) a sword.
Praying to Allah is the proper way.
As one's age moves beyond forty,
Not to harm others is the proper way.

Forty-five looks like a ridge of mountains and hills.
Looks like a sword sharpened,
Also looks like flood waters cresting.
But rapidly it changes.

At fifty his movements no longer are precise and nimble.
Getting on in years he no longer can climb high places.
He avoids the proximity of young people.
He is old and he himself admits it.

At age sixty a man is as if tied down with a rope,
No longer bothers to button the chest of his coat.
Molar teeth are loosened from his mouth,
Fried flour for him is the only bread.

Age seventy is said to be like glue.[8]
"My kneecaps and my waist!" are groaning with pain.
From his home he cannot walk far.
He makes rackets with his children and his wife.

Seventy-five is an age like a spring drying up.
Like wild flowers wilted next to that spring.
Everything is arranged by Allah. What else can you do,
But leave alone your old woman, joined by God's will?

While he reaches eighty, his hands and feet are trembling.
White beard and mustache are shaking as well.
He cannot pass the threshold—for example.
"Support me with your hand, my Old Woman!" he says.

At the age of ninety, man becomes thinner,
Like a thrown-away backbone.
His head starts quaking,
Like a rotten egg.

Without special grace given by God,
No-one can reach a hundred, I think.
If your age reaches that height,
You lack strength to even look at your tracks behind.

First these ages take away your eyesight,
Then your teeth and your words,
And then your knee bone and your waist.
At last the day comes that will take away you as well.[9]

Notes

1. The happenstance that this story rationalizes the absence of the camel in the Kazakh calendar is obvious. The Kazakhs are Muslims and would have included the camel rather than the unholy pig. But the Chinese calendar was older than the presence of Islam in China, and was well-nigh universal as far as Chinese culture has reached.

2. The Chinese dragon, *lung*, is *ulyw* in the Kazakh calendar. On the whole, the Kazakhs are unclear as to what this dragon might be. They simply accepted the Chinese custom of naming a year after the dragon. But as pastoralists they have neither accepted nor understood the ancient Chinese deity of agriculture and rain. In contrast, Kazakhs recognize the fierce dragon, Aidahar, who lacks the cloud and rain attributes.

3. The Kazakh people by and large, and nowadays, do not know what the designation *meshin* means—if they ever did. According to the Chinese calendar this animal should be Monkey.

4. Collected by Li Zengxiang during winter of 1956, from Tokhtasyn, a Kazakh herder in Shaghantoghai county, Tarbaghatai prefecture.

5. From Mukhtar Äwesov. *Collected Works*, vol. 16, p.42. Alma Ata: Writers Publishing House of Kazakhstan, 1985.

6. The colorful scarfs or *sawkele* are decorated with silver coins that produce tingling sounds.

7. From the Altai region, the home of the first author.

8. It sticks to you and you cannot move.

9. From the files of the Peoples Publishing House in Xinjiang.

Chapter 10

Death and Mourning

On joyous occasions, such as births and weddings, the Kazakh people intone happy songs to the sounds of a dombra. And when misfortune strikes, or when a loved one dies, that same dombra accompanies dirges of sorrow and mourning. Songs of lament are sung by members of a family when someone in the family dies. They are sung by clan members when some revered person, a headman of the clan or tribe, departs. They may even be sung if the deceased "person" happens to be a beloved horse or a hunting eagle.

Kazakh funeral speeches and songs may be divided into three types. There are (1) speeches for announcing that someone has died, (2) speeches for consolation, and (3) other speeches that are recited, or chanted, to mourn the fate of a deceased.

Speeches That Inform About a Death

The person who is asked to announce the occurrence of death is generally an older man, or a mullah. The messenger visits the relatives of the deceased and recites the sad news in rhythmic phrases or sentences. However, if someone has died at some distance from his *awyl*, the announcer must not report the news first to the relatives. He is expected to inform the elders of the settlement first. After having been notified of the tragedy, the head elder assembles additional older men and together with them he informs the dead person's nearest kin.

The announcer should be a man with good and resourceful manners of speech. He may not come right out and tell the tragic news. In the Kazakh view, spilling the news of a fatal accident quickly to the victim's kindred amounts to a display of ignorance and bad manners. It signifies the absence of humane feelings and is considered to be rude. Relatives should be informed gently, so as not to be driven into despair. Announcers should say first something ambiguous and then, gradually, add factual allusions.

A Kazakh story, which may have been based on a real event, can explain this custom better than a general description.[1]

Long, long ago, there lived a headman who ruled the Naiman tribe, a major division of the Kazakh people. His name was Tölegetai and his son was Khytai. The latter grew up and got married to Töke's daughter, Anar. Töke was a big chief of the Üsin tribe.

Back in her parental home, Anar used to live like a daughter and like a son. Therefore, when she got married she asked her father to give her the hunting eagle named "Khulash Ker" which her father loved very much.[2] Anar herself had trained that eagle. How she did this we do not know. In any case, occasionally it happened that this falcon did not stay with its task of hunting. Sometimes it flew back and attacked its human master. To be ready for all eventualities, Anar asked people to weave a twig basket for her, so that if the eagle would attack her she could cover herself with the twig basket and therewith avoid being harmed.

One day a group of young men, chieftains' sons, invited Khytai to go hunting with them, with his falcon. Khytai did not listen to his wife Anar's advise. He went hunting with these young men. They did not find any prey along their way and, therefore, in order to enjoy the sight of seeing them soar, they set their eagles free. The other birds circled in the air for a while and alighted on top of a mountain. Only Khytai's falcon turned back and attacked the head of its master. The young men who were with him threw themselves toward Khytai and covered the falcon's head with their coats and so carried the falcon away. But Khytai himself breathed his last.

After discussing how to communicate this misfortune to Khytai's family they chose an elder, named Aiman, to notify them about the death. The others followed him to Khytai's *awyl*. Aiman said to Anar:

Come Anar, my age-mate.
For what reason have we come to see you?
We are as frightened as a spirit who lost its family.
We meet you here.
A poplar tree cut off in the middle,
You cannot stand it up even with gold.
Water of a river muddied from its source,
You cannot clear it, not even with mercury.
People cannot die with a dead one,
A dead man cannot be revived.
Is it a spirit, or a demon,
Who has slashed his sword into our hero?

I am here, because I do not know what else to do.
I came to tell you personally.
It is my fault, I have not accepted.
I have not believed what you said.
And I have become severed from my good friend.
I want to stretch out my hand but cannot reach him.
(From regret) I am biting my own fingers.
I drifted away from my mind.
On an unlucky day we carried eagles.[3]
We loosened him from the clasp of eagle claws.
Can it be continued, still,
That life which has ceased?

We lost a friend, who is your darling,
I make known to you, now, that truth.
How can I cool your anger?
How can I dispel your agony?
There is only one way,
Chop off my head to soothe your anger.

After Aiman had so reported the death of Khytai, he threw his sword before Anar, squatting on the ground and sticking forth his head toward Anar—asking her to chop it off. But Anar had already fallen unconscious. The people sprinkled water at her and prayed to Allah to drive away the bad spirit that had overcome her. Slowly she regained consciousness. When she had come to full awareness she said:

> People say the hour of death never comes openly.
> Has this not been in an open way?
> People say that things taken away by Heaven
> Will never be given back again.
> Why should we still cry?
> I do not want to chop off your head.
> I do not want to curse you to cool my anger.
> When the hour of death comes,
> Neither you nor anyone else can escape.
> Who can stop the bullet of the hour of death?
> I do not want to cool my anger on your life.
> A vibrant life has passed away,
> Even if I die for him, he will never return.
> May Heaven protect us,
> Protect his four young children.
> I beg our Protector, Oh Heaven!
> What will happen to our father-in-law,
> He is old and his eyes are troubling him. . . .

After discussing the matter they decided together to ask a hero, Khazhyghaly of the Arghyn tribe, to inform Khytai's father, Tölegetai, about the misfortune. Khazhyghaly was a distant relative of Khytai's father, of the same generation. The next day, in the morning, Khazhyghaly entered Tölegetai's yurt with tears in his eyes, together with the other people. He was too uncertain to know what to say. So he said:

"Oh! You get up quite early?"

"My dear Brother, why do you speak with such a bated breath? It is not I who got up so early. It is you who came so early. Why do you come so early with so many people? It appears as though something has happened," said Tölegetai.

Regardless of the consequences, Khazhyghaly poured out the death announcement which he had prepared:

A man has a dromedary.
To him it is the most precious animal.
Ahead of the camel run tailakhs, and botas follow.[4]
Four children he loves equally.
That dromedary has been lost sight of yesterday.
Destiny has determined how it should be.
The reason for the hour of his death
Is the butterfly whom he himself has fed.
Those people who are gathering here,
Do not dare to tell you, afraid of trouble.
We (you and I) are the same age and in a similar situation.
To comfort you, that is why I came,
That is the task for which I came.
People sent me to let you hear.
The misfortune is for all of us the same.
The people's spines are bowed.
To all of us it is the same, even though he was yours.

The agony of this announcer expressed in rhythmic sentences, and the sympathy of the mourners, do speak for themselves. Kazakh emotions are intense and are profoundly reinforced by their poetry. Instead of explaining these matters by compiling general descriptions, it is much easier to quote another death announcement and to permit it to speak for itself. In this instance a famous man has died, and these are the words which were spoken to inform his son:

A mighty lion has fallen,
Who can give his life for him?
A rolling river has dried up,
Who can fill it with water?
Khans and sultans have passed away,
Who can give life to them again?
Your great-grandfather is Dajyrhan.
Kazakhs and Mongols,
Their disputes have been resolved.
Your grandfather is Khyjymhan,

His enemies saw him and trembled.
Your father is Baishuwakh,
He has fallen from his golden throne.
The people who sit here are afraid
To tell you about his death.

Beisenghaly's account may be supplemented with an 18th Century death announcement preserved in poetry:

An occurence of death is reported not only to close relatives, but also to the deceased's headman and friends, especially if the deceased is a wellknown person. So for instance the death of Bögenbai, a famous Kazakh hero during the 18th Century, was reported to Ablaikhan by a famous bard *(akhyn)* named Ümbetei Zhyraw.[5] After that bard had recounted the relationship that existed between Ablai and Bögenbai, during various battles and social crises, Ümbetei said:

Oh Ablai! Ablai!
Please continue to listen to my words:
One whose age is slightly more than yours,
Whose name is greater than a high mountain,
Your intimate friend from youth,
While you grew up he was your age-mate,
Being now just a little over eighty
He has turned away his head and left this world.
Your hero passed away—Bögenbai.
Loyal to his faith he prayed while breathing his last.
Several times he called your name.
"Give my regards to him," he said thrice,
He regretted not having seen you.
....
Please stop the tears in your eyes.
Speak a good blessing for your friend:

And here follows the blessing:

"May much happiness accrue to you,
May your child sit on the golden throne.
May your child live as long as Bögenbai,
And be a hero just like Bögenbai.

May good fortune follow that hero,
May his people live in peace and harmony.
May the Creator help him.
Let him shine high in Heaven."[6]

Samples of death reportings, presented here as translations of memorable poetry, pertain foremostly to members of the Kazakh aristocracy. It is therefore understandable why these announcers placed a great emphasis on characteristics like honor, victory, and superior prowess. They did this to underscore the tragedy of the event in pointed contrast to the deceased's earlier vitality and stature, yes, but also to memorialize that stature.

To a somewhat lesser degree that same ethos prevailed among the common people. Obviously, the death of a lesser person was noticed by fewer people, and seldom by those on high. It was therefore generally ignored by professional bards who earned their livelihood by way of flattering the aristocracy. The death of a commoner affected fewer people and, for that reason, elicited less high-flown eulogistic poetry.

But the announcer of a death in Kazakh tradition, at all status levels, was expected to mention the good deeds of the deceased, his contributions to Kazakh society, his friendships and his personal achievements. After having spread his preliminary cushion of poetic empathy, an announcer was obliged to inform about the cause of death and the deceased's last words, if these were known.

Words of Consolation

After having reported the news of a death to relatives and close friends, the announcer and the other people who have come with him all speak some words of consolation. Such words of sympathy are expressed to the immediate relatives and to close friends of the deceased. Everyone who comes to visit the family of the dead person will speak some words of comfort to the bereaved, and each one does it from his or her own perspective and degree of relatedness.

Words of consolation do range into the realm of poetry. Yet, as poetic expressions they remain freestyle. They may be short and they may be long, depending on the desire and ability of the one who does the consoling. The shortest can be a single sentence, and the longest can be several tens of lines. Here are some samples of single sentence expressions:

May Allah bless him!

May he go to Heaven!

May the place where he rests be as soft as silk!

May he attain the fulness of perfection!

Longer consolations are generally composed, remembered, and spoken in rhyme. Even though in the composition that follows the rhyme has gotten lost through translation, this sample is a typically lengthy consolation:

There is not an eagle whose plumes are whole,
There is not a steed whose hooves are whole,
There is not a camel whose fur is whole,
There is not a mare whose mane is whole.
The (rising) sun is not without its setting,
The (setting) sun is not without its rising.
No coal can last and burn forever,
No heart can live forever without distress.
Life is not eternal,
There is no iron that cannot be bent.
Think about it:
In this world,
For someone not to die is impossible![7]

The human repertoire of rational consolations is actually quite limited. There is only so much, and little else, that can be added by way of comfort in the presence of death. Nevertheless, there is a bounty of feelings that emanate from the poetry of mourning. And these personal feelings are far more impressive than all the rationality that might or might not be present in spoken consolations.

The Poetry of Mourning

Mourning songs for the dead may be sung by female relatives, such as the mother, wife, sisters, sisters-in-law, wives of father's brothers, daughters, and daughters-in-law. These songs may originate with the women themselves. But their words may also be composed by male relatives and given to the women to be sung as laments.

Another type of mourning poetry may be recited by men—to a dead relative or friend, to a beloved horse that has died, or to a lost hunting eagle. We shall first present samples of the women's mourning songs. And after that, for comparison, we will add some recitations by the men.

* * *

After a person has died, his or her female relatives sit together at the left side of the yurt, singing laments and weeping all the while. Each woman holds a handkerchief for wiping off her tears. Sometimes one among them leads with the song while others join and sing along. Sometimes one or the other sings solo. Female guests, when first they come to visit the bereaved family, embrace the matriarch of the family and join her to sing a song of mourning. These tunes are all set at a low pitch. They are chanted with grief and thereby express the women's state of mind. Inasmuch as the women sing and cry simultaneously, the entire scene erupts with utmost grief and sorrow. Not only are the women crying regardless of whether or not they are singing, the men who are in the yurt are weeping along with them. Mourning songs are sung for the dead, intermittently, for an entire year until all the offering rites *(nazyr)*, have been performed.[8] Our first example is a mourning song for a dead father:

> The beginning of words is Bismillä (In the name of God),
> What follows is the name of Allah.
> My father, the pilgrim (*khazhy*, hajji) has left this world,
> His age is ninety-two.
> Outside the door is a mountain slope,
> Flood waters run down from that hill.
> Hajji Papam has left our world.

The tears of my eyes become a lake.
You were prosperous and happy,
Next to you are your descendants.
You sat on your throne of power (became a leader),
At your age of seventeen.
You were a pilgrim [hajji] at sixty.
To the people you were like the spring season.
The people mourn for you,
Because you were a just *khazy*.[9]
One of your children is away to study,
As (precious to you as) the white and black of your eyes.
To see him while you were still alive,
Oh, it was not possible!
My Pilgrim Father *(Hajji Ata)*, patron of our people.
Your wisdom is out of the ordinary.
Orders came from Allah,
Which no-one can resist.
You were the support of our people.
About the loss of you everyone feels grief.
May Heaven be kind to you!
May your seat be in Heaven![10]

While the preceding song was an expression of a group, other
Kazakh mourning songs are often chanted from specific perspectives or
points of view. A bereaved daughter may mourn the death of her
mother as follows:

Once I wore a skirt made of silk,
You let me fly forth from the nest.
Yesterday you were still alive, my dear Mother,
Why did you have to leave this world so suddenly?
Before our door stands a red cliff,
I want to climb over it, but the path is too narrow.
My dear Apashym![11]
I wish to see you one more time.
There is a sail boat on the water.
We cannot ponder about this world.
Apashym, you have left us.
I am left behind, mourning!

You never slept at ease,
Always thinking about your pony (child).
While awake you always thought about your pony.
During the night you awoke four times.
You knelt beside the cradle to nurse your pony.
In the horse-herd is a mare with white hooves.
The horsemen feed her with great care.
Dear Apashym you are full of iman,[12]
You never slapped my head,
You covered me with my coat.
I lay before you and slept.
My dear Apashym, during daytime
I sat on your shoulder.
We are servants of Allah,
Who can break the lines which He has drawn!
You left your children behind.
You went, never to see again their cheerful gaiety.
Let me wipe the tears from my eyes.
My heart is full of grief.
I hope to leave this world
And for our spirits to be together.[13]

A song of mourning, chanted by a bereaved wife and addressed to her husband, may express sentiments such as these:

I start my words with *Bismillä*,
I disperse my grief with tears.
My Sabaz, be full of iman,[14]
Now please, let me pray for you.
In the midst of your gallant and vigorous years,
Death came to you as lightning.
How merciless is the hour of death!
Your age just came to fifty, Oh!
I cannot remain anymore in this room.
But I am reluctant to die.
My fate is different from yours,
Left behind by you, It is a pity!
In the mountains lies a yellow meadow,
Children are playing over there.

You cannot see your five sons grow up.
Oh! Your life has been cut too short.
The black-brown horse is left alone,
Saddled, ridden, and saddle belts streaming with sweat,
She has no older or younger brothers,
Who love her as dearly as you do.[15]
You were the protector of my life,
My heart is full of grief.
When the hour of death shall come to me,
I hope our spirits will meet again.
Oh! The sun rises slowly.
Oh! The sun sets slowly.
Oh! I lost you, my Sabaz.
May the place where you live be Heaven.[16]

A mourning song lamenting the death of a son, sung by women and the deceased's mother, may go like this:

Allah gave you to me.
The hour of death has overtaken you.
I feel it has been less than a day,
Even though you are eighteen years old.
In my heart you have a special place,
At our home, my Dear, you grew and roamed freely.
You grew up in our wide yurt, my Pony,
And now you are lying in the grave.
The word "child" is sweet.
The word "death" is full of grief.
People are coming back from the graveyard,
My Pony, how can you remain lying there?
Let my song of mourning be an ode of praise.
May the tears from my eyes provide light for you.
How many children can I have?
Who can be compared to you, my Pony!
Oh, the sun rises slowly,
And Oh, lost in the fog it sets!
My *Jetkinshe*, you passed away.[17]
Oh! May the place you stay be Heaven![18]

A song which women, together with the mother of a deceased daughter, may choose to lament goes like this:

Twelve years have passed
As if they were a dream.
Why has the hour of death come so suddenly?
Who would have known it?
Your eyes were shining like those of a camel's calf.
Your banged hair waved nicely,
Calling "Mom" you flew into my arms.
I used to kiss your forehead.
Wood of the pine tree is useless for a saddle.
Gold melted cannot be stone.
When I think about you, my Pony,
Even honey no longer tastes sweet.
Since my youth I was plagued with grief,
Exasperation never leaves my head.
Why is there so much grief for me?
There is more grief than hair on my head.
Evergreen trees have bowed their heads.
My voice breaks forth with *oibai* (O My!).[19]
How many *oibai* have I cried!
Where can one find her, she who is dead?
Tasjargan can break rocks,
My dear Child, you broke my heart![20]
In this world I will never see you again!
Wait for me in the next, my dear Child![21]

A mourning song on behalf of a deceased older brother, chanted by a woman, may express the following sentiment:

The hour of death comes suddenly,
How many unfortunate ones are devoured by it!
Extending forth its merciless sharp claws,
It always first takes away the lives of the poor.
From Muhammad who was the friend of God,
His life, too, was taken away by death.
From Ali whose sword dripped with blood,
His life, too, was taken away by death.

You who brought me up, my dear Brother,
Your life also has been taken by death.
Let me dishevel my black braided hair,
And after dishevelling I will braid it again.[22]
Every day I will stretch forth my angry hands,
To soak them in a pool of blood.[23]

In this manner Kazakh women in mourning express their grief for deceased persons whom they loved and respected. Most mourners accept the death of a person as a fate decreed by Allah, in Heaven.

*   *   *

What Kazakh women express in melodies of lament, and what they sing while a flood of tears chokes their voices, the men sometimes cast into a mould of poetic recitation. Poetic speeches can serve as a moderate means by which men express their grief. Such well-crafted speeches may be recited at the death of a relative, a famous person, or even at the loss of a horse or a hunting eagle. If the relationship of the deceased personage to a man has been very special, such as in the case of an only son or daughter, the father's relatives are expected to compose a poem of lament. When a distinguished person dies, professional male bards are asked to create the mourning poem that is to be recited at the funeral.

However, mourning poems recited by men are not as strictly limited to funerary occasions as are the laments of the women. Theirs may be offered in other suitable contexts as well. Poems spoken by men for a dead person are usually composed by a close relative of the deceased. In the case of beloved animals, such as a horse or hunting eagle, they are written by the rightful owners themselves. But inasmuch as the demise of animal friends does not require a formal funeral ceremony, poems composed on their behalf are not always recited in public. Sometimes they are shared quietly with other people.

The famous Kazakh bard, Bukhar, has composed a poem for mourning the death of Ablaikhan.[24] Ablai was the last khan of the Kazakh Middle Horde. While he ruled he bravely and unceasingly fought the Junkagir aggressors. To improve the life of his people he expanded their economy and instituted many social reforms. Bukhara composed a poem in four lines which summarized and exalted Ablai's great achievements. He thereby gave voice to the feelings of many Kazakh people:

> Oh our Khan! You let us sleep sweetly.
> Oh our Khan! You let us pasture without having to guard.
> Oh our Khan! You let us marry without paying dowry.
> Were we to send three men from three *jüz*[25] to die for you;
> We cannot save your life, our Khan![26]

Bukhar, the bard, composed another mourning song for the Kazakh hero, Ablai:

> Khabanbai comes from Kharakerei,
> Bögenbai comes from Kanzhyghaly,
> The hero Janibek comes from Kerei.[27]
> Another bard is Khazybek.
> The Middle Horde has people as the forest has trees,
> From them came four pillars.
> All of them are your roost (*tughyr*),[28]
> As you are the chief of eagles.
> At horse races luck was with you,
> As you yourself are the winged steed.
> They blasted cliffs and built paths for you,
> In the deep Tarbaghatai Mountains.
> They set up yurts for your soldiers,
> Next to Borly Lake.
> They gave vigorous counterblows to the Kalmuks,
> Fiercely mauled and pursued them to the Akhshaw Mountains.
> From your land they drove them out,
> Made pastureland for the Naiman tribe.
> Oh! Those heroes have left us, went away,
> They have left their homelands as well.
> If we fail to cry, who will cry?
> Why should tears not flow from our eyes?[29]

Aside from his sentiments for Ablai, we learn from Bukhar's lament also some historical facts about four famous heroes of the Middle Horde, and their tribal affiliations. We learn about their reputation among the remaining Kazakh tribes, and about their roles in battles against Mongol intruders.

A poem from another region, and an unknown poet, laments the death of a wealthy man, a *bai*. A rich man is defined by what he owns and does. His riches and lifestyle are being described in the process:

> Our bai is a wealthy man of six generations,
> When he moved about, six camels carried his loads.
> He caught young eagles from forested mountains,
> He trained falcons among mountain cliffs.
> Half of the year he hunted red foxes,
> He bought clothes for everyone.
>
> His silks are as plentiful as sheep wool,
> His riding horses are covered with blankets.
> Drinking water is being carried from mountain ravines,
> Mountain slopes are covered with his horses.
> Every year he held horse races.
> Oh, he was our sun, our moon, and our bazar.[30]
>
> Allah sent us misfortune,
> Our looks and appearances have faded,
> When we lost our khan.
> We lost our bazar within a day.
> Even though it is spring time,
> The eyes of the sun are clouded.
> Our falcon has left us and has passed on.[31]

Mourning the Death of Animals

A Kazakh proverb insists that "songs and horses are the two wings of the Kazakh people." With these they soar.

Earlier in this book we have explained the special status of horses in the Kazakh political, economical, and cultural life. Accordingly, there are many songs, poems, and epics that are recited in praise of horses and horsemen. When a beloved horse has died, or has gotten lost, its master often vents his feelings by composing a very personal poem of lament. Thereby he remembers the animal's physique and demeanor, its style of walking and its spirit. He commemorates the mutual love that existed between him and the animal. He contemplates the relationship which has been broken. Here is an example:

How strong he was, my brown stallion!
For him I traded eight horses.
No such horse can be found in the market.
Because no such horse is being born into this world (anymore).
My dear Red One, you ate to put on muscles and flesh.
Without such support, who can be prominent?
The people say that being jealous is not a good sign.
My enemies felt envy because I had you.
My dear Red One, you are of my sister-in-law's dowry,
And then you became my companion.
Riding on you I galloped.
Urystem, be blind! He saw you several times.[32]
Dear Red One, you were my life.
How lovely you looked, fleshy and muscular.
In a race with eighty-eight horses
You won the prize of forty meters red cloth.
The muscles on your buttocks are as large as tubs,
The hairs of your mane are as thick as *kerege*.[33]
Your four legs are strong with power.
Why have you dropped from the mountain like an invalid?[34]

What from among the poems of lament by men still remains to be presented is a mourning poem for a lost hunting eagle. Of all the Kazakh hunting methods, hunting with the help of an eagle is the most adventuresome and most cherished. Eagles and falcons are excellent for hunting foxes, and fox skins are used for sewing the best of fur coats. By Kazakh valuation, hunting with eagles is an act of bravery. Moreover, hunting with eagles is frequently considered to be a sport of wealthier than average men. When a hunting eagle dies it frequently happens that its owner will compose a poem of mourning. The poetic lament portrays the eagle's bold and powerful attributes, and cherishes the bird's memory:

208

Kazakh Traditions of China

As an eaglet I captured you in the Altai Mountains.
By training you became a bold and powerful eagle.
On a snowy day I carried you out hastily, to hunt.
I lost you and had to return home empty-handed.
To search for you I went to the Sawyr Mountains,
Blisters I raised on the back of my brown horse.
I enlisted help of Eseghasy, Khazybek, and Baikhara clansmen,
People who are adept in hunting.
I was afraid you might have been forcibly taken by others,
Afraid you might have gotten hung up on tree branches.[35]
I told Kärzhan and Mustapa,
To take care of you when they go to Turghut.
But, as one's wife will be cold to you some day,
So a man can also lose his eagle, or his steed.
We must thank Allah who gives us these.
He gives all these, and more than these again.[36]

Wives, eagles, and horses remain after all in Allah's hand. He gives them and takes them away. He is free to replace them, as well, in greater numbers than before. With this calculation of probabilities it becomes obvious that the mourning poems addressed to a dead or a lost horse, or an eagle, are after all a little less weighty and personal than laments chanted for a deceased member of humankind.

Notes

1. The account which follows here has been collected from Beisenghali, a herder, in Dörbilzhin County of the Tarbaghatai prefecture, Xinjiang, in 1988.
2. *Khulash* means the length of two arms, and *Ker* indicates brownish color. Thus the name refers to a large brown eagle.
3. Perhaps it was a Tuesday, the day of the week which traditional Kazakhs considered unlucky.
4. The camel is accompanied by offspring: two-year-olds *(tailakhs)* and yearlings *(botas)*.
5. Ümbetei Zhyraw (1706–1778). Ümbetei learned much from his father. While Kazakhs were at war with foreign peoples, he sang praises to the heroes.

Ümbetei was befriended with Bukhar and considered him his teacher. Ablaikhan (1711-1781) was a famous khan from the Middle Horde. An *akhyn* is an itinerant bard who travels from *awyl* to *awyl* to recite epics.

6. See Nyghymet Myngzhanyi, ed. *Khazakh Zhyrawlarynyng Zhyrlary.* Urumqi: People's Publishing House of Xinjiang, 1987, pp. 156f.

7. Collected from Beisenghaly, a herder, in Dörbilzhin County of the Tarbaghatai prefecture, Xinjiang, in 1988.

8. *Nazyr* refers to three offerings which traditionally were given to the dead on the 7th and 40th day, and also at the first anniversary, of their death. Nowadays money is given to the host family which, in turn, is expected to prepare a huge meal.

9. *Khazy* is a judge within the tradition of Islam.

10. Collected from Beisenghaly, 1988.

11. *Apashym* means "Beloved Mother." *Apa* means mother; *-shy* is a suffix which expresses love; *-m* is a suffix to indicate possessive first person singular.

12. *Iman* refers to Islamic perfection—submission to Allah, faith, devotion, and piety which, together, elicit God's mercy or grace.

13. Collected from Beisenghaly, 1988.

14. *Sabaz* is a respectful form to address one's husband.

15. Just as "Pony" is a term of endearment for children, so the widow here thinks of herself as the beloved dark-brown saddle horse that has been left abandoned by her deceased husband. The reference to older or younger brothers should be understood in terms of the *ämen'ger* tradition in marriage. See above.

16. Collected from Beisenghaly, in 1988.

17. *Jetkinshe* is a respectful term for addressing one's son.

18. Collected from Beisenghali, 1988.

19. *Obai* is an exlamation which in English approximates "O My!" or "O Dear Me!" Compare: "Obai, our enemies are coming!"

20. *Taszhargan* is a variety of grass that grows from crevices in rocks.

21. Collected from Beisenghaly, 1988.

22. When immediate relatives have died, women express their grief by putting their hair in a state of disarray.

23. Collected from Beisenghaly, 1988. From the contents of this dirge we know that the older brother of this mourning woman has been murdered. She wants to avenge his death.

24. Ablaikhan's original name was Abulmansur. Ablai was the name of his grandfather. Between 1711 and 1781 a Kazakh khan waged war against the Junkagir armies. Abulmansur joined the battle and bravely attacked the enemies. While fighting he shouted "Ablai," his grandfather's name. He won the battle and cut off the head of his enemy. From then on the people called him "Ablai."

25. Three *jüz* or "hordes"—formerly the pastoral Kazakhs were divided into three territorial groups or hordes—the Great, the Middle, and the Small. The Great Horde included Sar, Usin, Khangly, Dulat, Alban, Suwan, Zhalajyr, and other tribes. The Middle Horde consisted of Kipchak, Arghyn, Naiman, Kerei, Khongyrat, and others. The Small Horde contained the three tribal confederations of Jeti Ru, Alym uly, and Bai uly.

26. From "Poems of Kazakh Poets of Past Ages," Urumqi: Publishing House of Xinjiang, 1987, p. 231.

27. Kharakerei, Khanzhyghaly and Kerei are tribes which belong to the Middle Horde.

28. A *tughyr* is the sitting-roost for a hunting eagle.

29. From "Poems of Kazakh Poets of Past Ages," Urumqi: Publishing House of Xinjiang, 1987, pp. 217f.

30. *Bazar*, refers to markets which are bustling with activity and life.

31. From the files of the Folk Literature and Art Society of China, Xinjiang branch, at Urumqi.

32. Urystem is the archetypal horse thief.

33. *Kerege* are thin wooden stays or palings over which the felt covers of the yurt are spread and by which these covers are supported. The wood stays are obviously mentioned here as hyperbole.

34. From the files of the Folk Literature and Art Society of China, Xinjiang branch, at Urumqi.

35. There is a sheath of strings attached to the legs of a hunting eagle. These might get hung up in tree branches.

36. From the files of the Folk Literature and Art Society of China, Xinjiang branch, at Urumqi.

Glossary

Abai—Arghyn statesman; his full name is Abai Khunanbai; his Islamic name is Ibrahim

Abdal Kerim Khan—the Islamic name of Satukh Bughra Khan

Ablaihan, Ablaikhan—famous Kazakh khan in the 18th century, of the Middle Horde

Abulmansur—Ablaihan's original name

Abyi—a tribe belonging to the ancient Saks

Agha—address for older brother

ahyret—the hereafter, the other world, sometimes the netherworld; the same Kazakh word also refers to the white linen shroud into which the dead are wrapped

Airan—a clan belonging to the Naiman tribe

aitys—antiphonal songs, a poetic dialogue sung between two sides; between groups of men, men and women, boys and girls

akh—the color white, milk

Akhsai—a Kazakh autonomous county in Gansu province

akhsakhal—a venerable elder

akh söile—"please speak some words of good fortune"

akh süjek—noble, literally means "white bone;" the opposite of "khara süjek" which refers to commoners

0akhty—of milk

akhty bolsyn—milk is plentiful

Akhymbet—a clan of the Naiman tribe

akhyn, akhyndar pl.—bard, bards

akhyn aitys, akhyndar aitys—antiphonal songs of the kind recited by Kazakh bards

Alaköl, Ala-köl, Ala Kul—lake in eastern Kazakhstan, east of Lake Balkhash

Alani—ancient ethnic group living in Central Asia; in Chinese records they appear as ancestors of the Alchin and are named Yan Cai

Alash—legendary first ruler and patriarch of Kazakh tribes

Alban—tribe belonging to the Great Horde

Albat—a small clan of the Kerei tribe

Alkhambek—a place in the Altai region

Allaberdi—a clan of the Naiman tribe

Allahakpar!—Islamic prayer exclamation: God is greatest!

Almambet—a clan of the Naiman tribe

Altai—a mountain system in western Mongolia and eastern Xinjiang

Altyn Taw—a mountain range along the northern edge of the Kunlun system, defining the southeastern edge of the Tarim Basin

Amu Darya—a river flowing from the Pamir mountains into the Aral Sea

Apa—address for mother apashym—a beloved mother; Apa means mother; -shy is a suffix which expresses love; -m is a suffix to indicate possessive first person singular

aram—tabu, a word derived from Arabic

arbaw—invocation, means to invoke and to lure, to conjure, to seduce, and to mediate

Arghyn—a tribe belonging to the Middle Horde

Arkhalykh-title of a Kazakh epic featuring a hero by that name

Aryimassap—a tribe belonging to the ancient Saks

ashamai—a special saddle made for children, in the form of an "X"

Askhatagh—a tribe belonging to the ancient Saks

Assalawmaghalaikum!—Peace be with you! an expression derived from Arabic

Assyi—a tribe belonging to the ancient Saks

Ata—address for father, grandfather, an aged man; the designation also implies the quality of being great, grand, ancient

awhaw—a call for luring cows

awyl—a Kazakh settlement (aul) of four to five interrelated families of the same tribe or clan.

azhal—death

Äke—address for father; also used by a firstborn to address his or her paternal grandfather

Älim-uly—a tribe belonging to the Small Horde

ämen'ger—a betrothal arrangement which, upon death of the bridegroom, transfers the latter's rights and obligations to his brother

ämjin—Amen, a prayer ending

äwlije—an immortal; a celestial or supernatural being, a divinity, deity, or god.

baba—forefather; the designation also implies the quality of being great, grand, or ancient

Baghanaly—a clan of the Naiman tribe

bai—a rich man; someone who has substantial prestige and wealth

Baikal Lake—lake in southern Siberia, north of Mongolia; largest fresh water basin in Eurasia

Baisyjykh—clan of the Naiman tribe

Baitory—clan of the Naiman tribe

Bai-uly—tribe of the Small Horde

Bajeke—place name in the Altai region

Bajys—clan of the Naiman tribe

bakhsy—shaman, shamanic healer; a religious practitioner who operates on the basis of an archaic worldview; one whose services are employed to ward off, or defeat, the plots of evil spirits

Balkhash Lake—fresh water lake in southeastern Kazakhstan, east of the Aral Sea

Baltaly—clan of the Naiman tribe

balykh—fish

Barkol—a Kazakh autonomous county of the Hami (Kumul) prefecture, Xinjiang; "Balikun" is the Chinese pronunciation

bata—a blessing, a prayer

batyr—a hero or heroic warrior

bawyrsakh—small pieces of deep-fried bread

bazar—market, a general term referring to markets which are bustling with life

bädik—chants used in shamanic healing procedures

bädik aitys—antiphonal songs related to bädik

bäle zhala—misfortunes

bel—belly

bel khuda—a prenatal marriage agreement which becomes effective if the children, betrothed in the womb, are of opposite sex

besik—cradle

besik toi—the cradle ceremony, celebrated after the first forty days of the baby's life

besik zhyry—cradle song

bet, bet ashar—face, uncovering the bride's face during the wedding ritual

bij—headman of a hundred families

bijkem—young lady, respectful form for referring to a grown-up girl

Bilezik—place name in the Altai region

Bismillä—a Islamic prayer phrase meaning "In the name of God"; an expression to commence various types of activities

biz—we, the polite form for I

bota—a young camel, a yearling

botash—while "bota" means young camel; "-sh" is a suffix expressing affection and love

Bögenbai—name of a Kazakh hero

Bölekei—place name in the Altai region

börik—a round cap made of lamb, fox, or other animal fur

Bukhar—famous Kazakh bard of the 18th century

Bukhara, Bokhara, Boukhara—capital city of a West Asian khanate by that name; at one time this city was a holy place for Islam second only to Mecca

Bukhash—place name in the Altai region

Buratala, Buertala, Boratala—Mongol Autonomous Prefecture, Xinjiang

Buroltoghai—county of the Altai Prefecture.

Buwra—clan of the Naiman tribe

Caspian Sea—Inland salt lake, east of the Black Sea and south of the Ural mountains.

Chaghatai Horde—Chaghatai (Chagatai) was the second son of Genghis Khan and the territory assigned to him was Transoxiana, the area between the Amu Darya and the Syr Darya rivers

Chu River—a river in southeast Kazakhstan; it flows from the Tianshan mountains westward to a small lake in the dessert

Dahyi—a tribe belonging to the ancient Saks

delbe—a disease which affects horses; afflicted horses bite each other's necks and backs

Dolandy—a place in the Altai region

dombra—a two-stringed musical instrument of the lute family

dönen—a horse three years old

Dörbilzhin—name of a county and a river in the Tarbaghatai prefecture

Dörtuwyl—clan of the Naiman tribe

Dun Huang, Tunhuang—town in western Gansu

duwgha—prayer, word derived from Arabic

Duwlat—proto-Kazakh clan in the Ili, Chu, and Talas river valleys; identical with Dawlu Duwli, Duwlugh, Daluw, Duwleghas, Dalugh, Dughlat

Ebinor, Ebi Nor, Ai-pi—salt lake in western Dzungaria, northwestern Xinjiang

Elata—clan of the Naiman tribe

Emegeiti—a place in the Altai region

engbek, engbek zhyry—work, working songs

Ergetekti—clan of the Naiman tribe

Ermegeiti—place name in the Altai region

Ertis—name for Irtysh River; used in this book to signify the upper reaches of that river.

Ertory—clan of the Naiman tribe

esik—door, gate

esik köriw toi—"köriw" means look, see; "toi" means ritual; ritual for getting to know the house-door of the bride

Esimbek, Esimbek Batir—title of a Kazakh epic, featuring Hero Esimbek

Etil—the Volga river.

Farghana, Fergana—region west of Tianshan mountains, overrun by Arabs in 719, conquered by Chengis Khan and Tamerlane, taken over in 1513 by the Uzbeks to become part of Kokand

Georgii—Russian traveller who during the Middle Ages went to Central Asia and Kazakhstan

gül—a flower

Idris—the Arabic and quranic name of the biblical Enoch

ije—owner

ijman—Islamic perfection, submission to Allah's will, devotion, and piety which together are rewarded by divine mercy and grace; a word derived from Arabic

ijnsan—"humankind," as constrasted with angels or spirits

Ijteli—one of the twelve large clans of the Kerei tribe

Ili, Ile—river that flows from the Tianshan mountains into Lake Balkhash; name of the Kazakh Autonomous Prefecture, in Xinjiang

Isti—clan belonging to the Duwlat tribe

etkinshe—a respectful form to address one's son

Jissedon—tribe belonging to the Saks

Juchi—Genghis Kahn's second son

Kang Ju—Chinese name for Sogdians; some scholars assume that they spoke a Turkic language

Kaspyi—tribe belonging to the ancient Saks; they lent their name to the Caspian Sea

Kelbugha—clan of the Naiman tribe

Kedirlik—place name in the Altai region

Kerbugha—clan of the Naiman tribe

ker—brownish color

kerege—thin wooden stays of palings over which the felt covers of the yurt are spread and by which these covers are supported

Kerei—tribe belonging to the Middle Horde

Ketbugha—clan of the Naiman tribe

khagan—a khan with aspirations to command all three Kazakh hordes; the highest authority in the traditional Kazakh order

khaghanat—a kingdom or "empire" consisting of more than one horde (zhuz) ruled by a khagan

khaida—where, which place?

khaida barsa—anywhere one goes

Khairaghan, bäle-zhala——misfortune, bad luck

khairakh—a grindstone

Khalmakh—Kalmyk or Kalmouk, their ancestors are named Ojrot, speaking a language belonging to the Mongolian family; during the 10th century they roamed near the source waters of the Yenisei river, in southern Siberia; Zhungarians were associated with them

khalyng—numerous, thick

khalyngdykh, khalyngdykh toi—fiancee, wedding rite at the groom's home

khalyngmal—engagement or betrothal agreement; generally involving a dowry to be paid to the parents of the bride in the form of livestock and other goods

khalzha—refers to butchering a sheep for a woman who gives birth; it also refers to the meat that is prepared on her behalf

Khambar Ata—the deity who protects horses; another name for Zhylkhyshy Ata

khan, khanat—king, kingdom; a khan rules over a kingdom or horde (zhüz)

khara—black color

khara süjek—literally "black bone," the common people, the general population of Kazakh commoners (compare *akh süjek*)

kharsy khudalykh—two families exchanging daughters to become daughters-in-law in each others families

khazhy—a pilgrim or hajji who has performed the rites and has completed a pilgrimage to Mecca

khazy—someone appointed by Muslim authorities to preside over an Islamic judicial proceeding

khez kuwar—a national game, played between girls riding on good horses against boys riding on bad horses; the girls are permitted to strike the boys with their whips

khoishy—shepherd

Khoishykhara—a man's name

khongyr—brown color

khorkhakh—timid, cowardly, chicken-hearted

Khorkhyt Ata—a 9th and 10th century famous Kazakh bard, composer and actor; he is known as the father of Kazakh and Turkic music; his tunes are mostly sorrowful laments

khoshakhan—intimate call to lambs

Khosmurat—a man's name

khozha—a descendant of Muhammad; an owner or headman; a Muslim or mullah who is skilled to perform circumcision

Khuwbas—a horse's name, literally Thinface; thinfaced horses, with little flesh on their faces, are considered to be good horses

khuda—relatives by marriage

Khudai—name for God or Allah, derived from the Persian "Huda"

khul—male slave

khulash—the distance measurable with outstretched arms

khulyn—pony, a young horse

khung—female slave

Khurban Ait—the Islamic holiday that commemorates the intended sacrifice of Ishmael, by his father Abraham; it is celebrated seventy days after Ramadan

khurt—dried hard cheese

khyjykh en—a sideways cut on a domestic animal's ear, made as a mark

khymyz—fermented mare's milk

khysyr—a mare that has not had a colt during the present year and that has not dried up in the course of the year

khyz—a girl

khyz uzatyw toi—the getting-married ceremony

Khyzyr—name of a benevolent celestial being with a white beard; he always brings good fortune in Kazakh legends

Kichi Zhüz—the Kazakh Small Horde originally included the following clan and tribal units: Älim-uly, Zheti-uly, Bay-uly. They spent winters along the lower courses of the Syr Darya and Ural rivers, also between Irgiz river and the Turgai mountains. They found summer pasture upstream along the Ural, Tobol, and Irgiz rivers.

Kipchak, Khypchakh, Kipshak, Kifshak—proto-Kazakh tribal confederation; the Chinese knew them as Kefucha, Qibuchawu, Gubishao and Qincha; in some European languages they are known as Quman, and in Russian as Polovtsi

Kirrilov—leader of a Russian expedition

Kiting—place name of the Altai region

Komar—tribe belonging to the ancient Saks

kök—blue color

kökpar tartyw—literally "gray wolf grabbing;" "kök" means gray, and "par" is derived from "böri" which means wolf; a competitive game played on horseback, identical with *lakh tartyw* (goat grabbing)

köris, köris ajtyw—songs sung by a bride, crying, before leaving her parents, brothers, sisters, and other relatives

Kök Tängri—Blue Heaven; has since ancient times been recognized by Kazakhs and other Central Asiatic herder tribes as the principal supreme deity

kösh—an exorcistic command which means "Get away!" "Get out!" "Move away!"

küshik küjew—literally puppy son-in-law, a man who moves in with his bride's family

lakh—a young goat, a kid

lakh tartyw—a national game, played by two groups of men on horse back; the object is to snatch the carcass of a goat and carry it to a point designated as goal; identical with *kökpar tartyw* (gray wolf grabbing)

mal—livestock

meshin—monkey

molda—mullah, a Muslim cleric

momyn—gentle and easy, to be taken in

mu—Chinese measure of a unit of land, about one fifteenth of a hectare

mukhaddas—sacred place, such as Mecca, Medina, and Jerusalem; a word derived from Arabic

nawryz—New Year, a word derived from Persian

nawryz közhe—a gruel prepared for New Years Day, made of rice, millet, wheat, dried cheese, meat, salt and water

nazyr—offering rites to the dead. Three offerings are given on the 7th and 40th day, and on the first anniversary. Relatives of the deceased ask a mullah to recite a passage from the Qur'an. The hair of the dead person's horse, its mane and tail, is cut and the animal is set free. A year later it is captured and butchered. The meat is cooked for the people who come to attend the first anniversary rite.

neke—to get married, marriage; betrothal gifts are given by the groom's family to the bride's family; mullahs recite verses from the Qur'an, thereupon the relationship between husband and wife is established

oibai—an exclamation which in English approximates "Oh My!" or "Dear Me!"

Oisil Khara—the divine lord of camels

ojykh en—a halfround hole cut into the ear of a domestic animal as an identification mark

Oraza Ait—the annual feast that celebrates breaking the fast at the end of Ramadan

Oraza ijman—refers to the faith expressed by celebrating Oraza Ait

Orta Zhüz—the Kazakh Middle Horde originally included the following clan and tribal units: Naiman, Kerei, Arghyn, Kipchak, Khongyrat, Wakh. The Middle Horde spent winters along the lower Syr Darya river. Summers they roamed among the upper ends of the Sarysu, Tobol, and Ishim rivers.

öltiri toi—engagement or betrothal ceremony

peri—female celestials or angels; derived from Persian

pir—religious leader, saint; derived from Persian

pispeks—a wooden stick, used to agitate mare's milk in the saba

pushait—a call for luring sheep

Pushykh—Short Nose

Qurban Ait—the Muslim holiday that commemorates the intended sacrifice of Ishmael by his father Abraham; it is celebrated seventy days after the end of Ramadan

Ramazan Ait—Ramadan; the month of the lunar year during which, according to the Qur'an's own testimony (Sura 2:185), the holy

Qur'an was first revealed to Muhammad by God; a month-long fast is held to commemorate this blessed event; no food, drink, or sexual relations are permitted from sunrise until sunset

ruw—a Kazakh clan or tribe; several ruw together make a taipa

ruwbasy—the head of a Kazakh clan or tribe

saba—a hide bag used to ferment and to keep mare's milk

abaz—respectful form to address a man of courage

sadakha—zakat; alms or donations required of the faithful in accordance with the five principles or "pillars" of Islam

salam!—an Islamic word of greeting, meaning "peace!"

Sarkhashyk, Sarykhashykh—Yellow Bitch, the name of a helping spirit of a shaman; "sary" means yellow and "khashykh" means bitch.

sarymai—butter

saryn—a tune; at weddings it means wedding songs, sung to praise the groom and to persuade the bride not to be overly sad

sawap—rectitude, equity; a good deed that counts as credit toward existence in the hereafter

Särsenbi, särsenbi kuni—Wednesday

säwkele—a Kazakh scarf for married women; if used as a bridal coronet, it is inlaid with precious stones and fitted with a piece of red velvet to cover the bride's face

seit—a female descendant of the prophet Muhammad

Seksek Ata—Father Seksek, the deity who protects goats.

Semirechye—the geographical region occupied initially by the Great Horde. These Kazakhs roamed in the Chu, Talas, and Ili river valleys and sought summer pasture in the Ala Tau mountains.

Sharyighat—Islamic law; this word appears to have been derived from the Arabic "shari'a"

shashyw—a general name for all kinds of foods suited for celebrating joyous occasions, such as biscuits, cheese, sweets and
bawyrsakh

sheshen—a man with fluent speech, able to negotiate disputes

shildehana—the rite of giving birth

shilten—forty shilten are Arab men who brought Islam to Xin
jiang; they were killed in battle and buried there

Shopan Ata—Father Shopan, the deity who protects sheep

shöre—a call to lure goats

shyraghym—shyrakh means lamp, light, and -ym is the first person
singular possessive case suffix; in this form it means "My Dear!"

siz—polite form for "you"

sündet toi—rite of circumcision

süyinshi—gifts given to a messenger who brings good tidings

syngsyma—weeping songs, sung when a bride leaves her parental
home; "syngsyma" is derived from the verb "syngsy" which
means to weep, or to cry

synshy—a man who has the reputation of being a special knower of
horses

tai—a two-year old colt

tailakh—a two-year-old camel

takhyja—a round hat

taszharghan—a variety of grass that grows from crevices in rocks

taypa—a unit consisting of several ruw

tazsha—literally means "little baldhead;" a contemptuous name or
insult

Täte—address for Sister-in-law; also used by a firstborn to refer to
his/her natural mother if the child has been given to the paternal
grandparents

Tevlelev—a Russian envoy who was sent to the Small Horde in 1731

Tianshan—mountain range extending between Xinjiang and Kirghizstan

tilik en—a vertical cut from the livestock's ear to the top, an identification mark

Tobawut—small clan of the Kerei tribe

Tobol—river flowing from the southeastern Ural Mountains into the Irtysh, at Tobolsk

toi—rite, ritual, ceremony

Toitughysh—place name in the Altai region

Tokhpakh—clan of the Naiman tribe

Tokhpan—clan of the Naiman tribe

Tokhtar—a man's name

Tonhayit—small clan of the Kerei tribe

Torghaity—name of a cave in the Altai region

torpakh—a small calf, six to ten months old

tozakh—hell; this term is used primarily in Kazakh folk literature, in preference to *zhahhannam* which is of Persian origin

Töbet—clan of the Naiman tribe

töige—a song of milking women sung to a mother sheep, encouraging her to let the milk flow for her lambs

Tölegen—clan of the Naiman tribe

Tölegetai—clan of the Naiman tribe

tört tülik—four kinds of livestock; "tülik" means livestock

Transoxiana-region beyond the Oxus, including Bukhara and Sam arkand; in ancient times known as Sogdiana

tughyr—the sitting roost for a hunting eagle or falcon

Turfan—geological depression in the northeastern portion of the Tarim Basin; a center of ancient kingdoms, several times destroyed

Tuwma—clan of the Naiman tribe

Türkesh—clan belonging to the Duwlat tribe

ukhykhty—authoritative and powerful

Ulinggir—lake in the Altai region

Ulu Zhüz—the Kazakh Great Horde originally consisted of the following clans or tribal units: Üsün, Khangly, Duwlat, Zhalajyr, Alban, Suwan. It was formed during the 16th Century in the Semirechye region.

ulys—an association of several taipa

Ulys—New Year festival day

ulysting ulys küni—"the first great day of the year;" at New Year's day, Nawryz, the Kazakhs greet each other with expressions of this kind

Umbetei Zhyrzaw—famous Kazakh bard of the 18th century

Urumqi—capital city of Xinjiang; Chinese pronunciation is "Ulumuqi"

uryn baryw toi—ritual for going to the bride's home secretly and quietly

Urystem—the archetypal horse thief

Ushkhurylystai—place in the Altai region

Üsün, Üsin—tribe belonging to the Great Horde

Wakh—tribe belonging to the Middle Horde

Wakhkerei—clan belonging to the Kerei tribe

wäzhib—obligations, duty; derived from the Arabic

Weiwuer—Chinese pronunciation of "Uighur"

Xiongnu—Chinese name for "Hun"

Zenggi Baba—Forefather Zenggi, the deity who protects cows

Zhalajyr—Kazakh tribe now associated with the Great Horde

Zhalpakh Tanaw—Flat Nose

Zhamal—Beautiful, Beautiface; frequently used as a name for women; derived from Arabic

Zhamankhara—a man's name

zhanaza—the ceremony held for the dead; specifically, this word refers to Qur'anic prayers recited for the dead

Zhanburshy—clan of the Naiman tribe

zhanerke—sweetheart

Zhankhuly—clan of the Naiman tribe

Zhanzhigit—clan of the Naiman tribe

Zhanys—clan belonging to the Duwlat tribe

Zhastaban—one of the twelve large clans of the Kerei tribe

Zhädik—one of the twelve large clans of the Kerei tribe

Zhäntekei—one of the twelve large clans of the Kerei tribe

zhar, zhar-zhar—sweetheart, sweetheart songs

zharapazan—fast breaking songs sung on the day of Oraza Ait, at the end of Ramadan

zhawshy bolyw—to be a matchmaker, matchmaking

zhelek—a scarf, fringed with tassels; the customary headdress of brides at weddings.

zheli—specifically refers to the rope stretched between pegs to tie up young animals

Zhemenei—county of the Altai region in Xinjiang

Zherhan—small clan of the Kerei tribe

Zheti-uly—tribe belonging to the Small Horde

Zhetkinshe—a respectful form to address one's son

zhibek, Zhibek—silk; also used as a girl's name

Zhijrenim—clan of the Naiman tribe

zhilik—a general designation for the twelve longbones in limbs of sheep, cows, horses, and camels

Zhilugur—the last khan of Karakitay

zhin—genie, demon, evil spirit; based on the Arabic word "jinn"

zhol—road, way, path

zhol bolsyn!—may your journey be safe!

zhuryn—weak, weakling

zhüz—a horde; a nomadic association of clans or tribes. The Kazakhs are divided into a Great Horde (*Ulu Zhüz*), a Middle Horde (*Orta Zhüz*), and a Small Horde (*Kichi Zhüz*).

Zhylkhyshy Ata—Father Zhylkhyshy, the deity who protects horses

zhyr—odes, hymns

zhyrtys toi—rite for the delivery of betrothal gifts

Bibliography

Amanzholov, S. Voprosy. *Dialektologii i Istorii Kazaxckogo Jazyka* (*Dialects and History of the Kazakh Language*). Alma-Ata: The Education Publishing House of the KazSSR, 1959

Anonymous. *Hudud al-Ghalam* (*The Regions of the World*), a manuscript. Chinese translation from the 2nd English edition, by Wang Zhilai and Zhou Xijuan. Urumqi: Institute of Central Asiatic Studies at the Xinjiang Social Science Academy, 1983.

Anonymous. *Istoria Kazakskoi Literatury* (*History of Kazakh Literature*). Alma Ata: Academy Publishing House of Kazakhstan, 1948.

Anonymous. *Zhigitke oner de oner oleng de oner* (*To a Young Man...*). Urumqi: Peoples Publishing House of Xinjiang, 1989.

Anonymous. *Zhongxijiaotong shiliao huibian* (*Materials from the Historical Records of Traffic between China and Western Countries*). Beijing: Zhonghua Publishing House, 1977.

Arabin, Khazymbek ed. *Khazakh Hyisalary* (*Kazakh Epics*), 10 vols. Beijing: Nationalities Publishing House, 1982-1990.

Arystanbekov, H.A. et al, *Kazakh Sovet Entsiklopediasy* (*Encyclopedia of Soviet Kazakhstan*) Alma-Ata: Book Publishing House, 1980.

229

Awezov, Muhtar. *Tangdamalylar (Collected Works of Mukhtar Awezov).* Alma Ata: Writers Publishing House of Kazakhstan, 1985.

Awezov, Muhtar, ed. *Khazakh Adebijetining Taryihy (The History of Kazakh Literature),* vol. 1, Folklore. Alma Ata: Ghylym Baspasy Publishing House, 1960.

Ban, Gu. *Han shu (History of the Han Dynasty)* Beijing: Zhonghua Publishing House, 1962.

Barthold, Wilhelm. *Zwölf Vorlesungen über die Geschichte der Türken Mittelasiens.* Hildesheim: Georg Olms Verlagsbuch-handlung, 1962. Chinese Translation by Luo Zhiping. Beijing: Social Science Publishing House of China, 1984.

Benson, Linda and Ingvar Svanberg, eds. *The Kazakhs of China: Essays on an Ethnic Minority.* Uppsala: Acta Universitatis Upsaliensis, 1988.

Chen, Yongling. ed. *Minzu Cidian (Dictionary of Nationalities).* Shanghai: Dictionary Publishing House, 1987.

Compilers Group. *Ci Hai Minzujuan (Encyclopedia, Volume on Nationalities).* Shanghai: Dictionary Publishing House, 1978.

Compilers Group. *Hasakezu Jianshi (A Brief History of the Kazakh Nationality).* Urumqi: People's Publishing House of Xinjiang, 1987.

Compilers Group. *Kazakhtyng Khyskhasha Taryihy (A Brief History of the Kazakh Nationality).* Urumqi: Peoples Publishing House of Xinjiang, 1987.

Derbisalijn, A. ed. *Oghuz-name, Muhabbat-name (The Oghuz and Muhabbat Epics).* Alma-Ata: Science Publishing House, 1986.

Feng, Chengjün. *Xiyudiming (Geographical Names of Xiyu).*

Expanded by Lu Junling. Beijing: Zhonghua: Publishing House, 1980.

Jian, Bozan et. al. *Lidai gezu zhuanji huibian (Compilation of Biographies of Nationalities during Past Dynasties)*. Beijing: Zhonghua Publishing House, 1957.

Kang, Tai. *Biographies of Foreign States*. Lost during the Wu Period but cited in Bozan Jian, above.

Khadyrbek Zhünisbaiev. *Orta Azia Men khazakhstannyng uly Ghalym dar (Famous Scholars of Central Asia and Kazakhstan)*. Alma Ata: Ghylym Baspasy Publishing House, 1964.

Khongyrtbajev, A. *Khazakh Folklorynyng Tarijhy (A History of Kazakh Folklore)*. Alma Ata: Ana Tili Publishing House, 1991.

Li, Zengxiang, "An Introduction to Turkic Studies" in *Tujue Yu Gailun*. Beijing: Central Institute for Nationalities Press, 1992.

Liu, Xu. *Jiu Tang Shu (History of the Tang Dynasty)*. Beijing: Zhonghua Publishing House, 1975.

Liu, Zhixiao. *Weiwuerzu Lishi (History of the Uighur Nationality)*. Chinese language version. Beijing: Nationalities Publishing House, 1985.

Mura (Legacy) a quarterly periodical. Urumqi: Folklore Society of China, Xinjiang branch.

Myngzhan-uly, Nyghymet. Compiler. *Khazakh Zhyrawlarynyng Zhyrlary (Historical Verses by Kazakh Poets)*. Urumqi: People's Publishing House of Xinjiang, 1987.

Olcott, Martha Brill. *The Kazakhs*. Stanford: Hoover Institution Press, 1987.

Ouyang, Xiu. *Xin Tang Shu (Newer History of the Tang Dynasty)*, 225 volumes. Beijing: Zhonghua Publishing House, 1975.

Radloff, Wilhelm. *Proben der Volksliteratur der türkischen Stämme*, 3. St. Petersburg, 1870.

Rashid, al-Din Fadl Allah. *Jami al-Tawarikh* (1247-1318), Chinese transl. of the Russian 1952 edition, by Yu Dajün and Zhou Jianqi. Beijing: Shangwu Press, 1983.

Shalghyn (Downy Grass), a quarterly periodical. Urumqi: People's Publishing House of Xinjiang.

Shughyla (Dawn), the Kazakh literature monthly. Urumqi: People's Publishing House of Xinjiang.

Sima, Qian. *Shi ji—Dawan Lie Zhuan (Historical Memoirs—Biographies of Farghana)*, 2nd edition. Beijing: Zhonghua Publishing House, 1982.

Su, Beihai ed. *Hasakezu Wenhuashi (A Cultural History of the Kazakh Nationality)*. Urumqi: Xinjiang University Press, 1989.

Svanberg, Ingvar and Linda Benson, eds. *The Kazakhs of China: Essays on an Ethnic Minority*. Uppsala: Acta Universitatis Upsaliensis, 1988.

Zhang, Xinglang. *Zhong xi jiaotong shiliao huibian (Materials from the Historical Records on Traffic between China and Western Countries)*. Beijing: Zhonghua Publishing House, 1977.

Zhanuzakhov T. "A Study about the Origin of the Name Kazakh" in *Zhuldyz (Star Journal)* 3, 1983.

Zhuldyz (Star Journal) a literary, socio-political monthly. Alma-Ata: The Writers Association of Kazakhstan, since 1928.

Index